ASSERTIVENESS
AND THE CHRISTIAN
The Key to Resolving Conflict
by Charles E. Cerling

Tyndale House Publishers, Inc.
Wheaton, Illinois

Unless otherwise stated, all Scripture quotes are
from the *Revised Standard Version* of the Bible.

This book was originally published under the title
Holy Boldness.

First printing, Tyndale House edition, September 1983
Library of Congress Catalog Card Number 83-50073
ISBN 0-8423-0083-X, paper
Printed in the United States of America

CONTENTS

PREFACE

Would you like greater boldness in your walk with Christ and your relations with others? Would you like to be a more confident person, a more positive person? How would you like to be more assertive?

Ah, you react to that last word. Assertive. Yes, you want to be more confident, positive, and bolder—but *assertive?* Many Christians react negatively to the very idea of assertiveness. They think it's wrong.

But the dictionary says that "bold," "confident," "positive," and "assertive" are synonyms. They all say essentially the same thing, although each has its own particular connotation.

Part of the problem is that many people think "assertive" means "aggressive." "If I assert myself with others," they would say, "that means I run roughshod over their feelings." Assertiveness in that sense is indeed wrong, but that is not the sense in which the word is used in this book.

"Being assertive" means you have confidence in yourself, a positive attitude about who you are and what you have to contribute to society. You have a holy boldness in your relations with others.

You see, Jesus was assertive. Look at his last night with the disciples before the crucifixion (John 13:1-18). As they ate dinner together, Jesus rose from the table, prepared himself, and washed the disciples' feet. Talk about an assertive move!

He did what was completely contrary to society's expectations for a leader, because he thought it was the right thing to do. That's being assertive.

On another occasion, he saw a woman in need. The woman was a Samaritan, which made it even more taboo for him to speak to her. Jewish society said, You don't talk to a woman, particularly if she is a Samaritan. Again, Jesus asserted himself in the face of rules that said he should do otherwise. He spoke with the woman, communicating to her God's love (John 4). That's what is meant by being assertive.

Another time, Jesus felt tired after a period of ministering to others (Matt. 14:22, 23). Of all things, he sent the disciples away so he could get some rest for himself. He asserted his own needs when it was necessary for him to do so. That's assertiveness.

Once as he ministered, people called to him to tell him his mother and brothers were outside waiting for him. Can you imagine how guilty that would make some people feel, keeping people waiting? What did Jesus do? He used the occasion to continue and illustrate his teaching (Matt. 12:46-50). That's assertive behavior. You do what you think is most appropriate in any given situation.

Assertiveness, then, means that you have the confidence you need in both God and yourself to do or say whatever is needed, but always in love. This means you are willing even to do what others might not approve or like, if you think it needs to be done. That is the Christian way to live, because it places responsibility for your life in your hands—where God originally put it.

How does an author come to the point of writing a book like this? I came to it for two reasons. As I worked with couples in premarital counseling, as I counseled teens in learning how to get along with their parents, and as I worked with couples in marriage counseling, I became convinced that many problems in life are communication problems.

That is, many problems and much unhappiness exist because people, for various reasons, fail to express (communicate) what they think, feel, and want to do.

People often do what they do not want to do because someone else has made them feel guilty, anxious, or ignorant about something. Engaged couples go further than they really want to sexually because they don't know how to say no. One spouse lives in fear of his partner's negative reaction because he doesn't know how to express his own needs. Teens live in real frustration because no one has ever taught them how to reveal to their parents their own needs, opinions, and desires.

But I also saw Christians tied in knots, suppressing their desire to witness for Christ because they did not think they had the right to express Christian opinions to non-Christian friends. They feared their friends' reactions. They felt inept in witnessing, full of anxiety, so they chose not to witness—just to feel guilty. Many principles of assertiveness training can help a person communicate the gospel more effectively without being overbearing or obnoxious.

This book is written with the hope that it will help Christians communicate more effectively in all areas of their lives, particularly in family relationships and in their Christian witness.

Because assertiveness training has to do with communication, you often think primarily of communication techniques. But when you think of communication, you need to think of more than words, tone of voice, and gestures. You need to think about what sort of person you are. Thus, as you explore this book, you will deal with common problems of living as well as communication techniques. The words you use to communicate express who you are, not just what you want to say.

As I write this book, I recognize, as do all authors, some great debts. First I need to mention Norm Wright. He is one of the most creative biblical psychologists in the field. His writings have been an immense stimulus for my own work.

My wife, Geri, has given me tremendous encouragement. Dwight Small deserves thanks for encouraging me to keep going when I thought I would never finish. Thanks go to Phyllis Biggs, who typed the manuscript for me.

ONE
Speak the Truth in Love

How would you respond in the following situations?

"What are you doing tomorrow?" a friend queries as you leave work Friday afternoon.

"Tim, Ralph, and I are going golfing," you reply. "We plan on teeing off at ten."

"Great," says your friend. "I'll join you since you have only a threesome. We'll have a great time together. Twin Oaks is sure a nice course. See you tomorrow at ten."

How would you respond?

At your monthly Christian education committee meeting, the chairman says to the committee, "I feel God is leading the church to begin a Christian day school." He then calls into the room a Christian school organizer to tell the board just how the school can be started. As he introduces the man, the chairman says, "I've prayed about this situation for better than a year, and I know God is leading the church in this direction. I want us to plan for a Christian school in our church for next fall."

How would you respond? Would you simply go along with him since he has prayed about the matter and "knows" it is God's will? Would you sit there silently, seething with anger at this obviously manipulative power play? Would you speak up and say that you and the rest of the committee need time to think about this—that such decisions should not be made by one person, but should be a response of the whole committee? What would you do?

You're talking with an elderly friend who lost his wife about three years ago. As he has done in the past, he talks about how much he loved her and misses her. But, he says, "I know where she is [pointing up], and I hope to join her someday." The thought immediately flashes through your mind, *You hope to join her! She was a Christian, and you can* know *you will join her only if you accept Jesus as your Savior and Lord!* But as you think, he continues his rambling, talking about the successes of his children at their different jobs, about his grandchildren, and about his own enjoyment of life as an eighty-year-old.

He has moved the conversation in a different direction, away from the witnessing opportunity you originally saw. How would you respond? Would you simply experience frustration because a good opportunity for witnessing is gone? Would you attempt to redirect the conversation to get back to the subject of his hope of joining his wife? Would you drop the subject entirely as a lost cause?

What would you do?

WHO MANIPULATES YOU?

Do you realize that each of us often manipulates other people to get his own way? The first two illustrations demonstrate ways that people can manipulate others. The witnessing illustration demonstrates how society can manipulate. Society tells you, "Don't talk about such personal, potentially offensive matters as religion." Often people don't give you a fair chance to state your opinions about what they want you to do. In addition, even if given the chance, many of us wouldn't give our opinions, feelings, or desires—even if what we're trying to express is our faith in Jesus Christ—because we feel it would somehow be wrong for us to impose on someone else (even though we let others impose on us).

Because everyone wants his own way in life, we all develop,

often unconsciously, ways to get things from others without getting into a disagreement. Many of these ways are really manipulation. Others manipulate you to get what they want, and you manipulate others to get what you want. In the end, many of your transactions with others are a cycle of manipulation, countermanipulation, manipulation, countermanipulation, and so on until at last one person runs out of tricks and finds it necessary to give in.

Often you manipulate others because you're afraid, as we all are, of getting ridiculed when you try to express your opinion. As a result, you develop ways of getting what you want without expressing your real desires. You say, "Hey, Eric, that fishing trip you and Kevin are going on next week sure sounds great. I took one like it last year. I really had a ball. You know, I haven't been fishing like that since last time. I sure do enjoy fishing." Then you hope Eric will ask you to go fishing. What you should say is, "Eric, if you have room for another person, I'd sure like to join you. Is that possible?" The direct, honest question makes you vulnerable to a blunt no, but it *is* honest. The indirect statement protects you, makes your friend uncomfortable because he might not know what you want, and is *not* entirely honest.

Besides, manipulative behavior hinders your relationships with other people. By asking indirect questions, you can often make people think they are under attack. To say to your wife, "How long before dinner?" can be interpreted as, "Why do you have to take so long to get dinner ready after I get home from work?" It harms your relationship.

More forceful forms of manipulation cause even greater problems. The friend who invites himself along to a golf outing, a tennis match, a ball game, or a day of fishing soon becomes a person you don't want to be near. You live with the dreadful feeling that he is going to spring something else on you.

When people trap you through manipulation, they make you feel guilty, ignorant, or anxious. For example, a friend asks, "How can you say drinking is bad when you've never tried it?" as he attempts to make you feel ignorant about your lack of drinking experience. Or a child says, "If you don't do it my way, I'll tell on you," creating in his friend a feeling of anxiety. And when I know that four people could play golf at once and we have only three, I feel guilty about telling my friend not to join us. What I do know, however, is that in the future I will attempt to avoid this person. Manipulation destroys friendships.

What other things happen when someone manipulates me? When someone makes me feel guilty, anxious, or ignorant, I am often angry with myself after I comply with his request. My anger often turns against him for dealing with me unfairly. I also feel as though I have been cheated. Even as I didn't like to play with cheaters in childhood games, so also I do not like to be around cheaters as an adult. I never know when I will be taken advantage of.

The answer is not more effective countermanipulation. You don't solve the problem by learning how to manipulate more effectively than the other person.

ASSERTIVENESS TRAINING

The answer to this problem is assertiveness training. Although this procedure has employed many non-Christian principles, when properly approached it is based very firmly on Scripture.

First, it recognizes the deceitful character of human nature ("The heart is deceitful above all things," Jer. 17:9). Even Christians are manipulators. Christ may make us part of his family, but we still live with habits developed as children. In childhood we learned how to get things from people without saying directly, "I want that. Could I please have it?" We continue to use those manipulative patterns throughout our lives unless we make a conscious effort to change them. Assertiveness training looks right at our deceitfulness and deals with it.

Second, Ephesians 4:25 says that you should "speak the truth" with your neighbors. Again, assertiveness training says, "Exactly!" There is no reason to use manipulation or countermanipulation. You should speak the truth with those around you, not speaking deceitfully and not being afraid to speak up at all. Of course, that is no guarantee they will like what they hear or do what you want, but at least they have heard your thinking. At least you are not reacting against them without letting them know why. Assertiveness training is designed to help people speak the truth more often.

Those of us who have grown up in the evangelical church have heard many missionaries speak about the lying that takes place in foreign cultures. They tell us that, in many cultures, people say what they think others want to hear rather than speak the truth. They do everything possible to avoid offending someone, even lying to accomplish their purpose. We've always been properly astonished that people would lie rather than offend another person, because lying is wrong. However, I've slowly come to realize that we Americans have developed an even more subtle way of lying. We lie by being roundabout (devious) in the questions we pose to people. Rather than ask a straightforward question, we ask many indirect questions, never letting others know what we really want. Or we attack people rather than the problems, overlooking our own shortcomings.

Assertiveness in witnessing grows out of your commitment to Christ and the implications of the Great Commission (Matt. 28:19, 20). As a Christian, you have been called by Christ to help make disciples in every nation. This means you have a message to proclaim, a message that might not receive a positive response from those to whom you present it. Nonetheless, you have a responsibility before God.

Since that is the case, you need to use the most effective tools available in witnessing. Assertiveness comes on the scene as an effective new tool in helping you present your faith in Christ. Many of the underlying principles show that you have far more freedom to discuss what God has done for you and can do for others than you ever would have thought possible in your dealings with others.

Thus, assertiveness takes your witnessing out of the realm of, "How can I slip the gospel into this conversation so they won't even notice what has happened?"—a highly deceitful but quite common practice among Christians—and raises it to, "Tonight would be a good time to discuss my faith with these new friends. At an appropriate time I will tell them I have something important to say and I would like their attention as I do it." This response means you are honest with your friends while at the same time you present in a much clearer (because obvious) manner what Christ has done for you.

Assertiveness means that you let others know your true thoughts, feelings, or desires about a situation. This is nothing more than being honest with that person. However, we need to make some important qualifications about the way you express yourself. You must do it in such a way that your message is not a threat to the other person. When by the tone of your voice, the gestures you use, or the volume of your voice you say to the other person, "This is what I want, and I'd better get it or else," that is not assertiveness, but manipulation disguised as assertiveness.

Assertiveness is straightforward conversation about your feelings, desires, or thoughts. You are not apologetic for what you want, either by the way you talk or by the way you act. If, as you make your desires known, you stare at the floor and draw little circles with your foot, you aren't being assertive. If you make elaborate explanations to justify your desires, you are not being assertive.

Assertiveness is a middle position between aggressiveness and nonassertive, or passive, behavior. For Christians, it is important to note that *assertiveness is not aggressiveness.* That is a common misunderstanding. Standing up for your thoughts, feelings, or desires is not aggression against someone else. Aggressiveness is when you use anger, sarcasm, a loud tone, threats, or other devices that make a person feel threatened, to get what you want regardless of the other person's feelings or desires. Aggressiveness is wrong because it reveals a lack of love in your relationship with the other person. An aggressive person abuses others rather than giving consideration to the fact that they might have feelings different from his own.

Similarly, assertive behavior needs to be contrasted with passive behavior. Nonassertive behavior often means simply that you don't express your feelings, thoughts, or desires even though you have them (and often know what they are). If often means going along with what another person wants even though you would prefer doing something else or you think that what the other person suggests is wrong. You give in because you don't want what you think will be conflict as a result of expressing yourself. Or it might mean that you make a mild objection, just to let the other person know you don't fully agree with what you're going to do, but then you do it anyhow.

Assertive behavior falls between these two extremes. It's a firm, polite expression of how you feel, think, or of what you want. At the same time, it must be a demonstration of respect for the other person. You make no attempt to belittle him or to have him do something against his will (unless, of course, he proposes something clearly illegal or immoral). But you also don't permit him to force his will on you. When things go in directions you don't like, you say so. You're neither a doormat nor a bulldozer, but a person who has opinions, feelings, and wants that others need to take into account.

These ideas helped me most in relating to my wife. I realized that many times I wanted to do something—like going fishing—but was uncertain of her response. To protect myself, I would question her about her upcoming plans. If she appeared busy, I would not ask about going fishing. Now I tell her just what I want, then say, "Would that work out or would it cause problems?" I actually find myself going fishing more than before, and we also both feel better about the times when I go.

In the long run, assertive behavior is better than nonassertive behavior. Most people use nonassertive behavior because it accomplishes what they want now. They don't want to be anxious or bothered, so they choose to be nonassertive. But few people recognize that nonassertive behavior now makes it difficult to accomplish long-term goals later. If you don't stand up to the bully now, tomorrow, and the next day, he will continue to harass you. If you don't state your opinion or witness now, you may not get another chance. Nonassertive behavior is counterproductive. It may get you what you want now, but it makes achieving your far-more-important future goals all the more difficult.

OUR GOALS

What, then, is the goal of assertiveness training? Is it to get your own way? Is it to make certain that everybody knows what you want? Not necessarily. The goal of assertiveness training is not to make certain that you get your way. If that is your understanding, you've missed the point. What we seek to accomplish is to let others consider your thoughts, feelings, or desires about a situation. If we do that, I'm convinced that many people will respond positively and alter their behavior. They will do so because most people want to get along with those around them, if only they know what they want. (I recognize that sin causes people to act contrary to this, but most of the time people attempt to get along with those around them.)

Finally, a goal of assertiveness training is to help you choose *how* you will act. Many people learn early in life that it is easier (in the short run) to act passively or nonassertively in relations with others. At the same time, they frequently have the feeling that there must be a better way than to be constantly anxious about their relationships with others. Others have learned that they can get what they want by bulldozing their way over others. But they, too, don't necessarily like what happens, because they know people fear them, and they don't like that. Assertiveness training attempts to help people learn how to choose the way they want to live. Giving a person tools to help him act assertively overcomes the nonassertive or passive person's anxiety. As he sees a better way than bullying others, the aggressive person learns how to communicate with others without intimidating them. As a result, each person should be able to evaluate a situation and choose how to be assertive if that would be appropriate. We will also see that *assertiveness is not always wise.*

Ultimately, assertiveness training is based on the biblical principle that *we, and we alone, are responsible for the way we act.* Because God is someday going to judge each of our lives based on the way we have lived, on the things we have done, we recognize that we are responsible for the way we live (Rom. 14:12; 2 Cor. 5:10). This is true of the Christian and non-Christian alike. Yet much of our language reveals different beliefs. We say, "I wouldn't have padded the expense account if everyone else hadn't been doing it"; "I would never have gotten involved with that woman if she hadn't dressed in such a provocative way"; or "I wouldn't have gotten angry if he hadn't mistreated me so." Each of those statements suggests you are not responsible for the way you act, but that is not true. And assertiveness training is a tool to help you act more responsibly more often. It is a means of helping you resist the manipulative influence of others on your life so that you can choose for yourself how you will act.

Assignment: Use the following tool to help you see how well you understand the difference between assertiveness, aggressiveness, and nonassertiveness. Circle the assertive answer; "x" out the nonassertive response; and check ("✓") the aggressive behavior.

1. Your wife says she will be home from shopping at 6:00 so that you can leave for an appointment at the office at 7:00. At 6:45 she pulls into the drive. You . . .
    a. Quietly help her with the groceries, saying nothing about your appointment.
    b. Help her with the groceries, but scowl and grumble the whole time without ever actually saying what is bothering you.
    c. Say, "What's wrong with you, anyhow? You promised to be home by 6:00. Doesn't your watch work?"
    d. Say, "I'm upset because you promised to be home by 6:00. Now I'll be late for my appointment, and Mr. Powers is a very important client. Next time, I would appreciate it if you could keep your promise."
2. You told the mechanic when he took your car for a tune-up that you didn't want the oil changed because you do it yourself. As you look at your bill, you notice that you've been charged for an oil change. You . . .
    a. Say, "What's the matter with your ears? I told you not to change the oil, but you did it anyhow. I absolutely refuse to pay this bill until you remove the charge for changing the oil."
    b. Say to yourself, *Anyone can make a mistake. Next time I'll make certain this doesn't happen by writing out the instructions.*
    c. Say, "I notice that you charged me for an oil change. When I came in this morning, I said I didn't want to

have the oil changed. I don't feel I should have to pay for that portion of this bill."

   d. Say, "Did I tell you to change the oil this morning? I don't remember. I don't think I did, but maybe I am mistaken. What do you remember about it?"

3. You spend hours during the summer getting your yard into shape. At last it's beginning to look the way you want it to. Your neighbor walks over and says, "You've got the nicest looking yard on this block. You should be proud of it." You respond . . .

   a. "Thanks, I appreciate the compliment. It's taken a lot of work, but I think it's worth it."

   b. "This? Oh, it's really nothing. There are others around here who have done as good a job."

   c. "It's really not much. You could make yours look just as good if only you would put some effort into it."

   d. "I'm glad you noticed. I do enjoy it, but it means so much more when someone else notices and can enjoy it also."

4. Your son worked long hours this past term on a special project at school. Today he brought it home. It really looks great. As you look at it, you . . .

   a. Say, "That's great, David. I really think you did a super job."

   b. Think to yourself, *Boy, I wish I could have done something that good when I was in school. It sure must give him a sense of accomplishment.*

   c. Say, "What grade did you get on that? Was it as good as the other kids did? I hope the teacher gave you what you deserved for it."

   d. Say, "Hey, that's not too bad. It could use a little more color, but that's not too bad."

5. Last January your boss promised you a 10 percent raise this year. It's now June, and nothing has happened. You are beginning to fall behind with some of your bills. You approach your boss and . . .

   a. Say, "I heard that Ralph and Albert got raises in their last paychecks. That sure was a nice thing for you to do for them."

   b. Say, "Last January you promised me a raise. I need it

because I am falling behind with my bills. Would you give me the raise?"

e. Say "Uh, if I remember right, and I don't always, you promised, at least I think you did, to give me a raise. I don't think I have, uh, received it yet. Is there, uh, anything you could do about it?"

d. Say, "Hey, last January you promised me a raise. I haven't received it yet. What kind of place is this, where no one keeps promises?"

6. As you talk with your neighbor over the back fence, he comments, "When I look at the mess the world's in today, I often ask myself, 'Is it really possible for anyone to be truly happy?' What do you think?" You respond . . .

a. "It certainly is. All you have to do is ask Jesus Christ to be your Savior and you'll be happy. He alone is the secret to happiness."

b. "You know, that's a good question. I've often thought about it myself. My answer might not be too great, but I think my commitment to Jesus Christ as my Lord and Savior gives me the secret of happiness."

c. "I think a person can be happy, Kevin. Although the world is in a mess, I've found that my relationship with Jesus Christ makes all the difference to me. And although I sometimes might be down for a short time, generally speaking, I'm happy."

d. "I would imagine that you would get a different answer to that question from each person you asked. Happiness is elusive. We search for it most of our lives without finding it. I think I've found the answer, but I'm not sure it would work for you. I think the answer is Jesus Christ."

Key to test:
Assertive answers: 1-d; 2-c; 3-d; 4-a; 5-b; 6-c.
Nonassertive answers: 1-a,b; 2-b,d; 3-b; 4-b,d; 5-a,c; 6-b,d.
Aggressive answers: 1-c; 2-a; 3-c; 4-c; 5-c; 6-a.

TWO
Your Bill of Rights

You alone are ultimately responsible for the way you act. That was our conclusion in the last chapter. It is a logical deduction from biblical statements that all people will one day be judged for their deeds, good or bad. In suggesting this, I in no way deny that salvation is by faith, but simply emphasize the clear biblical teaching that faith results in visible works (James 2:14-26).

If it's true that each of us is ultimately responsible for the way he acts, it's important for you to learn to recognize when people are manipulating you into doing things you really don't want to do. To do this effectively, you need to know the more common rights people violate when they manipulate you. In this chapter, we will discuss your "bill of rights" as a human being relating to other human beings.

NO RIGHTS FOR CHRISTIANS?

Many Christians, however, would challenge the very idea that we have a bill of rights. "A Christian should claim no rights," they would say. "We gave up all our rights when we committed ourselves to Jesus Christ. From that time forward we have no rights." So I ask the question, "Is it wrong for a Christian to talk about rights?"

First, let's remember the basic goals of assertiveness. I want to help you develop tools to guide your decisions about how you will act in any situation. We aren't talking about overwhelming others with no regard for their rights, but about choosing an appropriate way of acting that will help others know what you would like to have happen. Thus, my primary concern is that you know how to express your opinions, feelings, or desires to others so that they will have an opportunity to take them into account in what they choose to do.

Now let's look a second time at the question, "Is it wrong for a Christian to talk about rights?" To do this, let's examine the question by looking at its extreme opposite. Let's assume for a minute that a Christian has *no* rights. If that is the case, then when a man asks me for all the money I have, I have no right to withhold it from him. When someone takes my children from me, I have no right to resist. Obviously, we must assume that we have *some* rights. The problem is to determine just what rights we do have as people attempting to live with other people. I firmly believe that everyone has the following rights:

1. *You have the right to judge what is best for you and to be responsible for the consequences.* We will treat the two elements of this right separately, but we need to remember that the parts are inseparably bound to one another.

Remember, our basic assumption is that we are all responsible for the way we act in any situation we encounter. But you and I can only be responsible if we can choose what we will do. And if that is the case, then each of us has the right to judge what is best for himself. If you do not have the right to judge what is best for you, you can no longer be held responsible for the way you act, because freedom to choose and responsibility are two sides of the same coin.

Recently a neighbor put in a new patio at his home. Ray had to tear out the old one because it had cracked and torn loose from the foundation of his house. As he finished taking out the old patio, a number of friends made suggestions about the best way to put the new patio in so that it would not cause the same problems as the old one. It was obvious as Ray listened that he was becoming frustrated by all the advice. At that point I told him, "Ray, remember, you are the one who has to pay the bill, so the final decision has to be yours after we have all given our advice."

Advice from friends can be useful, but remember that *you* alone are responsible for your decision in each situation.

The second half of this right is equally important: You are ultimately responsible for the consequences of your decisions. If you decide to do something and it causes trouble, you are responsible to straighten out the mess. This means you can't blame others for the bad advice they give. You're the one who chose to follow their advice. Nothing compels you to follow another person's advice. Even in the extreme instance of having someone put a gun to your head and demand that you do his bidding, you can always refuse and suffer the consequences. There is nothing anyone can do short of actually moving your limbs for you that will compel you to do something against your will. As a result, you are always responsible for the consequences of your choices.

Assignment: Write out a recent experience in which you permitted someone else to determine what was right for you.

2. *You have the right to act without defending or justifying your actions to others.* Many people have a difficult time with this right, but it is simply a logical outgrowth of the first right. If you have the right to judge what is best for you, you must also have the right to act without defending or justifying your action to others. If you could only act when you had given a reasonable verbal defense of your action, there would be many times when you could not act as you wanted. You would be stopped by your inability to put into words a defense of your action. However, you have no need to defend your action to others.

In John 4, Jesus meets the Samaritan woman at the well and carries on a discussion with her about her salvation. When his disciples return from buying bread, they are astonished that he is carrying on a discussion with a woman and, moreover, a woman who is a Samaritan. But Jesus never justifies his action to them. He simply continues his discussion until the woman becomes a Christian. Had Jesus waited to talk with her until he could have justified his action to his disciples, he might never have talked with her at all. They were so blinded by prejudice against both women and Samaritans that nothing could justify such behavior to their minds. Nonetheless, Jesus acted. As our example, he shows us here (as well as elsewhere) that you have the right to act without defending or justifying your actions to others.

Jesus behaved in a similar way when he waited until three days after hearing about Lazarus's illness before traveling to Bethany to raise him from the dead. You cannot live your life responsibly if you have to justify your decisions to all who challenge them.

Even as I state this right, however, I recognize that explaining your actions to others often makes life easier for everyone. I'm not saying you should never explain your behavior to another, but that you don't have to. Too frequently, people decide to do something they would enjoy, a friend asks them why, and they quit because they can't give a good explanation. "I want to" is all the explanation that is necessary. That says that you have the right to act even though you cannot give a good reason for doing it.

Assignment: Write out a recent experience in which you did not do what you wanted because you couldn't defend yourself.

3. *You have the right* not *to conform to others' expectations for you.* Because most Christians are sensitive to the opinions of those around them, this right is important. You don't have to conform to others' expectations for you, even if that means they will think less of you. "Hold on now," says an objector. "The Bible says in Romans 14:15, 'If your brother is being injured by what you eat, you are no longer walking in love. Do not let what you eat cause the ruin of one for whom Christ died.' That means you shouldn't offend anyone! It may prevent God from working in that person's life." Many Christians think they should conform to the regulations others have for their lives, even though they don't really want to follow those rules.

I recently saw in my own life a small way in which I was conforming to expectations established long ago by my parents, even though I no longer agree with them. Every time we had spinach (which I cannot stand), I would put a little on my plate and eat it. I did that because my parents taught me that it's impolite not to eat a little bit of everything on the table. It suddenly dawned on me one day that here I was, living as an adult by rules established for children. I could say with equal authority that it's impolite for my wife to serve spinach when she knows I don't like it! But the sensible solution, since she likes spinach, is for me to pass it by while she eats it. That way we are both happy about the results.

Again, we need to look at Jesus' life. Did he conform to others' expectations for him? If we are honest, we must say he rarely did. In fact, his nonconformity is primarily what got him into trouble with the Pharisees. He didn't conform in matters he thought unimportant. Similarly, you need to choose the way you will live in accord with your understanding of what the Bible teaches. Admittedly, that will sometimes mean giving up something for the sake of another person, but that will be your choice. You choose to give up your right because you are concerned about another person. You do not mindlessly conform because you see no alternative.

As a minister, I frequently encounter this decision. There are things I do not think are wrong, such as going to see an occasional movie, but when I am with people who think these things are wrong, I don't talk about them. If I think they would be seriously injured in their Christian experience if they saw me do them, I choose not to do them. Movies are too insignificant to be the cause of another person's downfall, but not attending movies has to be my choice. It is wrong for me to conform simply because I am afraid of what others might think.

Assignment: Write out a recent experience in which you did something solely because you thought others expected it of you.

4. *You have the right to be wrong—and to suffer the consequences.* As you will note, this right also comes from your first right—the right to judge what is best for you and to be responsible for the consequences of your behavior. Given that right, you also have the right to be *wrong* and to suffer the

consequences. So long as you're responsible for determining how you will live, you'll make mistakes (that's true of us all). You'll sometimes make serious mistakes. Sometimes when you are about to make a mistake, a friend will warn you that what you are going to do either will not work or will get you into trouble. Although you must respect your friend's right to express his opinion, when he's finished, *you* have to decide for yourself whether you're willing to take his advice. If you decide not to take his advice, you open yourself up to making a mistake. But if you're going to be responsible for your own behavior, you need that right, even if it means you must suffer the consequences.

I find this an excellent learning device with my children. When I see them doing something I think will get them into trouble (but is not sin), I advise them of the possible consequences—then tell them to make the decision. Sometimes they surprise me by getting things done without getting into trouble. Other times they fail and learn the need to listen to others. In both instances they learn the lesson of being responsible for the consequences of their decisions.

Why is the right to be wrong so important? Because without it, you lose the right to determine what you will do. If you must stop and change plans every time someone points out that you will be wrong if you follow a particular course of action, you lose the right to choose how you will live. Only if you have the right to be wrong will you really have the right to judge what is best for you.

Why is this such a potent argument for most of us? Probably because warning is the method parents use to discipline. "If you do that, you'll break something" is a constant refrain of parental discipline. Now, as an adult, whenever someone suggests that your proposed course of action will lead to failure, childhood reaction comes into play and you stop. But that is wrong. You need the right to weigh the possible consequences against the benefits of your proposed action and then decide for yourself what to do, even if you're wrong. That is your right.

Assignment: Write out a recent experience in which you stopped doing something because someone told you it was a wrong decision.

5. *You have the right to change your mind.* This seems so obvious, but many people have difficulty changing their minds. They think others will think less of them if they do because they don't want to give up the image of perfection they have cultivated for years. But if you have the right to be wrong, shouldn't you also have the right to admit you were wrong and change your mind?

Recently, I mentioned to a friend of my congregation that I wanted to visit him that week. As the week progressed, I discovered I had too many other pressing things to do. At first I felt compelled to keep to my stated plan, but then I realized my plan was wrong. I admitted it, and I made plans to visit the next week.

Some people think it's wrong to change your mind. For them the ultimate insult is, "But you never did it that way before!" They assume that you don't have the right to change, that you never grow enough to move from immature to mature behavior. But from what we've seen earlier, if you have the right to act without defending or justifying your actions to others, you must also have the right to change your mind whenever you want to. Does that mean you are inconsistent? Possibly, but more likely it means that you have sufficient confidence in yourself to admit that you were wrong and to correct the wrong by changing your mind.

Furthermore, what does it mean to be consistent? Consistency has to do with your principles for living. You can't live by another man's principles or you give up the right to judge what is best for you. Consistency is living by the principle that you always choose what you think will, in the long run, be best for you. (For Christians, this question is settled by what the Bible teaches on the subject.) By that principle you'll be consistent, even though others might not agree.

Although the right to change your mind is a basic human right, the Bible points out one time when changing it is wrong: when you've made a promise even when you realize you will be hurt by keeping it. Once you've made a promise, you should live by that promise, even if it means you'll suffer as a result. It may be that you will want to talk with the person you gave the promise to and see if you can get out of it. But if the person refuses, you should live by your word. Of course, no one can stop you from changing your mind; but to break your promise would be sin.

Assignment: Write out a recent experience in which you did something you didn't want to because you thought it would be wrong to change your mind.

6. *You have the right to your opinions, feelings, and desires.*

"You shouldn't feel that way."

Has anyone ever said that to you? You've just experienced something unpleasant and reacted, when a friend comments, "You shouldn't feel that way."

Now, quite frankly, he might be right. You shouldn't feel that way, given the principles he lives by. But you do feel that way, and you have the right to your own feelings. Obviously, you suffer the consequences of having those feelings, but no one can deny the reality of them.

I recognized this a few years ago while fishing with my wife. We were wading in a fairly deep, fast-moving stream. The stream was full of fallen logs, making it an ideal fishing place, but difficult for walking. Because I have fished under those conditions on many occasions, I thought nothing of it, but I sensed on my wife's part a hesitancy to get involved. As we talked, I discovered she had fears about her safety. From my point of view those feelings were unjustified, but not from hers. I had to recognize her right to those feelings and take them into account, even though they were very different from my own.

This rule holds true in everyday conversation as well. Many Christians think they offend others if they give their Bible-based beliefs about the issues of life; as a result, they remain silent. They do not witness because they feel they have no right to impose their opinions on others. But each of us has a right to his opinions. Others might think them foolish; they might take offense at having to hear them; they might choose to reject them. But nothing another person does or wants can deny you the right to your opinion.

A few years ago I was requested by Parents Without Partners to present a discussion on sex and singleness. My theme for the evening was that although we cannot deny the reality of our sexual feelings, we have no right to express those feelings in an unbiblical way. Some members of the group reacted in anger. Nonetheless, I had the right to my opinion, and their opposition to it was no reason for me to remain silent. The Christian position has just as great a right—no, a greater right—to expression than non-Christian opinions.

You also have a right to your desires, as long as there's nothing sinful about them. If in the middle of the night you want a peanut butter and pickle sandwich, that's your business. If you like to sleep in the bathtub, that's no one else's concern.

But because this right has the greatest possibility for abuse, we need to introduce a note of caution. Just because you have the right to your opinions, feelings, and desires does *not* mean that you have an attendant right to express or fulfill them at any time or place. Common sense must temper your expression. You might feel like yelling "Fire" in the midst of a crowded restaurant as a practical joke, but that would be wrong. Your feeling is real; no one can deny its reality. But if you choose to act on it, others have the right (sometimes under law they have the obligation) to judge your behavior. The right to feelings, opinions, and desires must be balanced by the rights of others, and by your Christian love for them.

Assignment: Write out a recent experience in which you denied your right to have an opinion, feeling, or desire because of its unacceptability to others.

7. *You have the right to be treated as fairly as others.* This is the only right in our bill of rights that is not derived directly from the first right. It's inserted, however, because many Christians think that simply because they are Christians they're not entitled to receive equal treatment with others. It may be all right for a non-Christian to complain about poor service in a restaurant, but if a Christian complains, that would be a poor example for others; thus he grins and bears it. If my neighbor borrows my tools and never returns them, it would be all right to complain if I weren't a Christian, but because I am, I just have to suffer with his behavior. Com-

plaining would be un-Christian. When a contractor bills me too much for his services, I can't complain because that would not appear very Christian.

That attitude is wrong! You have the right to be treated as fairly as others. When something goes wrong, even though you're a Christian, there's nothing wrong with speaking up! You pay for the same sort of service in a restaurant that a non-Christian does. You deserve the same sort of respect for your property as a non-Christian, and if you don't get it, you have the right to refuse to loan your tools. If you're overbilled, you have a right to draw that fact to the attention of the contractor. There's nothing wrong with pointing out to someone that you don't like the way you're being treated.

A special word needs to be said about persecution. Many Christians think that when someone persecutes them by verbal abuse or mistreatment, they should grin and bear it. Persecution is simply their lot as a Christian. I'd like to point out how contrary to Scripture that attitude can be. In Acts 16:35-40, Paul had been thrown into prison, and when the authorities discovered he was a Roman citizen being held without trial, they attempted to release him without a fuss. But Paul demanded that they come and let him out personally. He demanded the same treatment any other Roman citizen would have received. Similarly, when the Jews had him jailed on false charges, he appealed to Caesar the same as any other Roman citizen could do (Acts 25:1-12). When he thought it would be helpful for himself or the church, he demanded and received fair treatment.

When you're mistreated because of your Christian faith and that mistreatment is illegal or against company rules, you do your persecutor no favor by simply accepting the persecution. Quietly but firmly, you should make it known that it is wrong and you want it stopped. Just because a person is a Christian does not mean he should be a doormat for every person who wants to mistreat him. Obviously, you need to exercise wisdom in choosing when to protest and when to be silent, but you need not think that silence in the face of persecution is the only option you have.

Assignment: Write out a recent experience in which you accepted mistreatment even though you wanted to complain.

LOVE BEFORE RIGHTS

Having discussed a human bill of rights, we need to look at responsibility. Our society is so concerned with rights that it often forgets that rights grow out of responsibilities. As we continue to discuss assertiveness, you'll discover that responsibility to others plays no small role. We might emphasize rights because they're basic to assertiveness, but we never want to neglect our attendant responsibilities. None of the rights covered in this chapter means you can run roughshod over others. None of those rights means you can violate the basic Christian law of love to others. When you begin to exercise your rights in ways that violate love, you're in the wrong. No right eliminates the responsibility of love.

Assignment: (1) Memorize the first four rights. (2) Write out examples of violations of those rights this week.

THREE
Your Responsibility

How can you be assertive without being obnoxious? How can you be assertive without at the same time running roughshod over others? Can you really emphasize your rights all the time without using others as a doormat? I believe you can, but only if you're careful.

Assertiveness is used by many people as an excuse to destroy others in a new, but socially acceptable manner. The book that popularized assertiveness training is, *When I Say No, I Feel Guilty.* When I first read that book I appreciated much of what I read, but I read with reservations. Obviously, assertiveness helps, but I kept saying to myself, "Do we have to be so mean in our dealings with others?" Many of the illustrations in that book suggest that an assertive person is an obnoxious person who walks right over the rights of others. More recent books have reacted against that idea. Even the title of a recent book, *Responsible Assertive Behavior,* shows that assertiveness training has been stung by criticism that it creates people who simply use assertiveness as another manipulative device to get their own way without any concern for the rights of others.

Christianity brings a perspective to assertiveness that isn't available in the non-Christian world. What is a Christian's first obligation in life? Jesus says in Matthew 22:37-39 that we are first to love God and then to love our neighbors as ourselves. Those are the greatest obligations a Christian has in life.

I began this book by suggesting that many people have learned how to get their own way by manipulating others. Many Christians have also fallen into this trap. I also showed, however, that manipulation isn't honest, that it tricks or pressures people into doing things they don't want to do but do nonetheless because of fear, anxiety, or feelings of guilt. Now I want to add that manipulation is in conflict with love.

You can't claim to love another person while you manipulate that person against his will into doing what you want. Thus, I suggest that every Christian has a responsibility in addition to his bill of rights. And that responsibility is to love your neighbor. Nothing you ever do in asserting your rights should in any way conflict with God's demand to love your neighbor.

But it must be pointed out that love and *nonassertive* behavior also conflict. Here is where many Christians have trouble. But isn't it true that when you are not honest with others about your feelings, opinions, or desires, you are failing to love them? When you refuse to permit the other person to know your relevant feelings, opinions, or desires you are judging that person incapable of dealing with them.

You are saying, "If I let him know this, he will not be able to handle it, so I'd better not let him know." As a result, you hide the information from him to protect him or to protect yourself from what you think would be his reaction. In either case, you have judged him (probably wrongly) as incapable of handling the revelation.

As a minister, I often see this nonassertiveness in the handling of family illnesses. A woman learns from her doctor that she has a serious illness, possibly cancer, that might require surgery. Instead of telling her husband, she continues to act as if everything is all right. She wants to keep him from unnecessary worry. She is afraid he might do something drastic if he learns of her illness. By keeping silent, she judges him incapable of handling the bad news. That is an unloving action.

THE TRUTH—WITH LOVE

Love for others, then, means a *careful* openness with them. Nothing in assertiveness training means you *have* to express

every idea or feeling you have to *every* person who comes in
contact with you *no matter what* the situation. But love does
mean that you have a responsibility to communicate to others
information that you alone possess that would be important
input into their decisions. If knowing how you feel or think, or
what you want, would have an effect on the way a person will
behave, you have the responsibility to communicate that information. That is love; it is also at the heart of assertiveness.

Think of the many times in your life when you have done
something only to discover later that a close friend wanted
you to do something else. Your immediate response was, "Oh,
if only I had known, I could have done what he wanted
without any trouble." If that is your response, think of the
many times when information you had might have changed
your friend's behavior, but since he never received your information, he did something you did not like. Love means you
give the information you have—your feelings, opinions, or
desires—so that the other person has an opportunity to decide what to do after considering all the information and not
just the limited amount he would have without your input.

Love means that your rights stop where the next person's
nose begins. That cliché suggests that you're free to do as you
want so long as your behavior in no way harms anyone else. In
contrast, our age emphasizes rights. You supposedly have the
right to do as you please. That statement is used to justify all
sorts of immorality and otherwise unacceptable behavior. But
whenever your rights are exercised at the expense of love to
another person, you are in the wrong, having gone beyond the
legitimate scope of your rights.

Thus, if your assertive behavior makes you generally obnoxious to other people, you have not properly understood
the meaning of assertion. You are instead an aggressive person who tramples the rights of others. Assertiveness is wrong
when it means hurting other people needlessly.

Assertiveness does not mean indiscriminately exercising
your rights. There are times and places when it's wise not to
be assertive. If your boss speaks sharply to you and you know
that he loses his temper easily, asserting yourself right when
he's already angry might mean you'll lose your job. If a man
points a gun at you and demands your money immediately,

asserting yourself to show him how much you dislike his behavior might cost you your life. There are many other instances far less severe when assertion would be irresponsible.

YIELDING RIGHTS

The logical conclusion is that responsibility to yourself and others sometimes means *choosing to yield your right to be assertive.* Helping you feel free to make that choice, however, is one of the basic goals of assertiveness training—it's not meant to help you get your way every time, but to help you evaluate each situation and then choose how you will act.

You might evaluate a situation and determine that the responsible thing to do is to yield your right to the other person. Is that not real love?

As Paul writes to the Corinthians (2 Cor. 11:8-10), he tells them that when he worked with other churches he asked those churches to support him. While at Corinth, however, he never made any monetary demands on the church, but allowed other churches to support him. He tells them that he did so because of his great love for them. Does this mean he loved the other churches less? Hardly! It simply means that Paul saw something in the situation at Corinth that made him choose to be supported by others while he worked there.

As we read the New Testament, we recognize that a person who works with a church is rightly in a position to demand a fair wage from the church. Both Jesus and Paul state that the laborer is worthy of his hire (Luke 10:7; 1 Tim. 5:18). Yet Paul chose in love to give up that right for the sake of accomplishing something at Corinth that would have failed had he chosen to exercise his right. That is what it means to be responsible and assertive. Paul knew what his right was, but he chose to yield that right.

A goal of assertiveness training is to help you evaluate the situations you find yourself in and make the right choice about how you should act. Many times this will mean actively letting others know how you feel, think, or what you want, but there will also be times when your evaluation will lead you to silence. You will see that as the most responsible behavior at that time.

The key element in all of this is choice. You need to be sufficiently free in your actions that you can choose from a wide variety of options the way you will act.

We can see clearly in Jesus' life such freedom of choice. At times he forcefully confronted the religious leaders because of their bull-headed unconcern for the needs of people. At other times, to help them grow, he patiently explained to people what he wanted from them. He could be both outwardly loving and kind or outwardly forceful and dynamic, depending on what the situation demanded. He wasn't bound by conformity to any preconceived pattern. Assertiveness is an attempt to help you develop the same freedom to choose to behave in a way that is appropriate to the situation.

As you have read this far, you have probably recognized that assertiveness is more than just a way of behaving. It's also a way of looking at life. For this reason, in some of the following chapters I want to deal with problem areas of Christian living.

What place, if any, does conflict have in the life of a Christian? Your attitude toward conflict determines to a large degree how assertive you will be.

What about anger? Where does it fit? Does it fit at all? Your attitude toward anger will determine how assertive you will be.

Do you often worry about what others might think or do? That also plays a role in your assertiveness or lack thereof.

And what do you think of yourself as a person? What psychologists call your self-image plays a major role in whether you are assertive.

Thus, while assertive behavior is a way of acting, it is also far more. It's an expression of who you are. As you become comfortable with who you are in the eyes of God, you will feel more comfortable with assertive behavior.

Having become comfortable with yourself, you'll be free to let others live by the assertive bill of rights, just as they should let you live by it.

Assignment: (1) Memorize the last three rights in the assertive bill of rights. (2) Write out examples of violations of those rights during this week.

FOUR
How to Change

Change! That's what we're concerned with. You want to begin to act assertively instead of nonassertively or aggressively as you have in the past. But how do you change?

The key to change is found in Romans 12:2, where we learn that change comes "by the renewal of your mind." Change in any aspect of your life comes as a result of change in the way you think. As a person thinks, so will he be.

YOU ARE WHAT YOU THINK

A crucial proverb in assertiveness says, "It's not what happens that counts, but what you think about what happens." Events affect different people in different ways. When we examine the people, the events, and the responses, we discover that people respond differently because everyone perceives the same situation in a different manner.

I recently read an anecdote about the late union leader Jimmy Hoffa. When he was in court one day, a man stood up and aimed a gun at him. How would you have responded? Screamed in terror? Dived for the nearest cover? Jimmy Hoffa charged at the man. He could see no answer to the problem other than direct action. Others would see the situation differently.

Why do people perceive the same situation differently and therefore respond differently? Each of us perceives differently because we all bring to the event different backgrounds that condition the ways we perceive. As a result, because no two people have identical backgrounds, we all perceive and respond differently.

Thus, it is our thoughts about what has happened played against the background of all our previous experiences that determine how we will act. What you think about what happens makes the difference. One man sees a gun pointed at him and freezes in terror. He thinks, *What's the use? There's nothing I can do. I might as well just stand here and die.* Another sees the same gun, thinks, *My only chance is to dive for cover,* and dives. Jimmy Hoffa sees the gun pointed at him, thinks, *If I don't get him first, he's going to get me,* and charges.

How does this relate to assertiveness? Many people think nonassertively or aggressively, and therefore that is inevitably the way they act. I can think of no better anecdote to illustrate that you are what you think than this: A salesman was driving along a country road late at night when suddenly one of his rear tires went flat. He opened the trunk of the rental car and discovered that the jack was missing. Thoroughly upset, he remembered a farm about a mile back down the road. Late as it was, he began to walk back to the farmhouse. As he walked he thought, *How lucky for me that this farmhouse is so close. I'll just knock and ask the farmer for a jack. He'll give it to me, I'll change the tire, return the jack, and be on my way.* But the farther he walked, the more the late hour bothered him.

Maybe the farmer won't like being roused at this time of night, he thought. *I'd better offer him a couple of dollars for his trouble.*

But as he continued to walk he worried further. *A couple of dollars really isn't much when you consider the late hour. Besides, he probably has to get up early to do his work. I'd better offer him five dollars.*

As he walked into the yard he thought, *Really now, five dollars isn't very much. I'd better give him ten.* Then he became indignant and thought, *Ten dollars! That sure is a lot of money for just getting out of bed and loaning a jack to a man with a flat tire!*

Arriving on the porch, he knocked at the door. The farmer opened an upstairs window and yelled down, "What do you want?"

The salesman looked up and yelled, "Ten dollars! What a skinflint! You can keep your jack and I'll keep my ten dollars, and I'll call a tow truck in the morning." With that he walked away.

That is the way many people think—nonassertively. They approach every problem in life as if it were a disaster. When they get finished talking to themselves about it, there is no way they will act assertively because they are convinced such action would lead to calamity. As a result, like the salesman, they walk away thoroughly frustrated, without any real idea of what would happen if they did act assertively. If you think assertively, you'll act assertively. You are what you think.

But it must be pointed out that you cannot *not* think bad thoughts. If you're looking at an event in your life, you can't say to yourself with good effect, "Now I don't want to think nonassertively." The moment you begin to think that you *can't* think nonassertively, you *will* begin to think nonassertively, because that is what you are concentrating on. The fact that you can't just empty your mind of negative thoughts is analogous to the illustration Jesus used when he said:

When the unclean spirit has gone out of a man, he passes through waterless places seeking rest; and finding none he says, "I will return to my house from which I came." And when he comes he finds it swept and put in order. Then he goes and brings seven other spirits more evil than himself, and they enter and dwell there; and the last state of that man becomes worse than the first (Luke 1:24-26).

Jesus is pointing out a basic principle of life: If you want to remove the bad, you have to replace it immediately with something good.

An illustration from India also shows that you cannot *not* think about something. A peddler was selling powder that he claimed would turn to gold when mixed with water. As he concluded each sale, he would lean close to the buyer and say, "This only works if, when you mix the water with the powder, you don't think of little red monkeys." Obviously, that is just what everyone thought about when they mixed the powder with water.

Our relationship with God illustrates this: Repentance means turning from evil *to God*. When a person repents of sins he has committed, he doesn't simply say he is sorry for what happened. True repentance means that a person begins with sorrow for sin (which even unrepentant people may have), and as a result of his sorrow for sin he turns to God to express his sorrow and seek forgiveness. He then commits himself to living by God's will. Simply to sorrow over your sin is to act like an unreformed alcoholic who is sorry about his drinking. He is sorry about what it does to himself, to his family, to his job, and to many other things, but his sorrow is useless because it does not result in a change of direction in his life. When we repent of our sins we must turn from our sin to God. In the realm of assertiveness, this means that you need to replace your bad thoughts with good thoughts. Let me suggest a plan of action.

PLAN OF ACTION

First, create a small card that you can put in your purse or pocket that has "STOP" written on it. Then every time you find yourself thinking thoughts that prevent you from acting assertively, pull out the card and look at it. If you're by yourself you should speak the word. STOP! That tells you that you can't just not think bad thoughts. You have to plan to replace the bad thoughts with good ones. In relation to assertiveness, this means you should think through an assertive plan of action and follow it.

The next step is developing counterthoughts against your nonassertive thoughts. Because your nonassertive thoughts are causing you to act nonassertively, you need to develop counterthoughts to challenge your nonassertive thinking. For example, the salesman told himself he needed to pay the farmer ten dollars to use the jack to change his tire. A good counterthought would be, *What would I do if someone woke me in the middle of the night with a flat tire? Would I be willing to loan him my jack? Certainly! Then why should I think the farmer will behave any differently than I would?* Or he might think, *Maybe the farmer will be upset, even charging me money to use his jack. Is that any worse than sitting up all night in the car until morning comes and I can get a tow truck? Even the truck driver will charge more than the farmer would to borrow his jack. I'll try and see what happens.*

No matter what situation you face, you have to develop counterthoughts against each nonassertive thought you might have. If you talk yourself into nonassertive behavior, you can talk yourself out of it and into assertive behavior by just challenging your nonassertive thoughts and replacing them with assertive thoughts. Developing believable counterthoughts is an important aspect of your plan to change. You might even want to write your better counterthoughts on the back of your STOP! card.

When I first entered the pastorate, I had negative feelings about my ability to work with young people. In one church in which we had several pastors on the staff, I even told the board I would not work with the youth because that was one of my major areas of weakness. But I have worked out counterthoughts that permit me to work with young people now. *I may not be the best man with youth, but I can do some work. I am probably average, but that means I do as good a job as most people.* With this attitude I go to work. It permits me to assert myself and do the job that needs to be done.

What next? How do you continue making your assertive plan of action? Write on the back of your STOP! card the right from your bill of rights that you permit others to violate most frequently. Then, whenever you sense that someone is violating that right, whenever you sense yourself thinking in such a way that you will let someone violate that right, pull out the STOP! card. After you look at the front, turn it over and read the right that you want to live by. Think about how you can put that right into action in the situation you face. It would also help to memorize or place on the back of the card an appropriate Bible verse you can review as part of the process.

All of this is designed to help you replace negative, nonassertive thoughts with assertive thoughts. As you change your thinking, you will also change your behavior.

In addition, you should undergird this whole process with prayer. Pray at the beginning about your lack of assertiveness. Pray when you feel you are having your rights violated. Pray as you make the attempt to be assertive. Pray about the possible need to yield your rights in love in a given situation. Although you change your life by changing your thinking, the real power to change comes as you permit God to involve himself in bringing your negative thoughts to light and giving you the strength to overcome them through assertiveness.

Many people, however, have difficulties at this point in the process. After a couple of days, they become discouraged because they see very little progress in their plans to change. And when they consider the large number of changes they want to accomplish, they give up because they think, *If I can't succeed with this one little problem, how will I ever succeed with all the others, particularly the big one?*

When you begin to think this way, you need to reconsider what change means. How can you know when you're changing? Should you expect instant and complete change like the alcoholic who, when converted, never touches another drop for the remainder of his life? No, change is rarely immediate; old habits die hard.

MEASURES OF CHANGE

Change is measured in three different ways, each important in its own right. The first measure of change is *frequency*. How often did you engage in your particular kind of nonassertive behavior before you began working on it? Once a week? Once a day? Ten times a day? If you engaged in this form of behavior ten times a week before, and this week you do it only eight times (managing to be assertive twice), that's progress. You're changing! What you want to see is a measurable change from one week to the next. You aren't looking for overnight perfection. So, figure out how often you did what you didn't want to before now, and see how many fewer times you do it during the coming week.

The second measure of change is *duration*. How long did your internal conflict over whether to act assertively or not exist in the past? Let's say that the last time your neighbor borrowed your tools without asking it took you a week to build up the courage to ask him to return them after you found you needed them. If this time you can ask for your tools five days after you discover the need for them, you're succeeding. Any time you can reduce the duration of your nonassertive behavior, you're succeeding.

Finally, successful change is measured by the *intensity* of the internal conflict. Let's say that you bought a sweater in which you found a flaw when you got it home. Last time this happened, you could think of nothing else for the remainder of that day and for the next few days, until at last you took it back to the sales clerk. If this time you purchase something defective and find that you can say, "I'll return it this Saturday and not think about it more than once during that time," you have succeeded in changing. The conflict about returning defective merchandise remains, but it is less intense than it was in the past.

Frequency, duration, intensity—these are the indicators of change. As you examine the areas in which you want to change, you have to determine how frequently you have engaged in the particular nonassertive behavior, how long it normally takes you to act assertively, and how intensely you experienced the conflict over whether to be assertive or not. When you have done that, you are then in a position to measure change at the end of the next week. You can look back and see if the behavior was less frequent, if the internal debate over whether to act assertively or not lasted a shorter (or in some cases longer) period of time, or if the debate was less intense than before. As a result, you can determine whether you are succeeding. These measures grant that change is rarely instantaneous and usually occurs over a period of time.

There is one final consideration in making a change—reward. Most people find it easier to change if they can plan a small reward for themselves when they succeed. For example, if I ask my neighbor to return my tools after five days, I can treat myself to a bottle of pop. If I worry only once a day instead of almost constantly and I return the sweater, I may treat myself to a shirt to go with the replacement sweater. The reward should not be big or you'll tell yourself you can't afford it. Some people give themselves rewards as simple as watching a half-hour television program. To be effective, rewards should be simple, inexpensive, and easy. They should also be immediate, since the closer the reward is to your successful completion of a task, the more inclined you are to succeed. So, plan a small reward for yourself when you have successfully changed according to one or more of the indicators.

Assignment: (1) Select an area of your life in which you want to act more assertively. Determine how frequently events arise in that area. Determine how long it normally takes you to act assertively. Determine how intensely you experience the decision-making conflict.

Now, create a STOP! card. On the back write the right from the assertive bill of rights that you see being violated in the situation. Put a Bible verse applicable to the situation on the back of the card, along with the right. Put down a good counterthought to your negative thinking. Use the STOP! card each time this week that the situation comes up. Note how often you use the card, how long it takes to resolve the conflict each time you use the card, and how intense the conflict is before you resolve it. At the end of the week, determine how much you changed during the past week. Remember, even a small change *is* change. If your problem occurred 1000 times last week and only occurs 987 times this week, you've improved. You are looking for change, not miracles.

In addition to the STOP! card, (2) plan a course of action to resolve the conflict. Write it out and keep it with you. Then you can use the plan during the week as your means of solving the problem.

FIVE
Conflict Is Good

Complete the following agree-disagree exercise adapted from Norman Wright's *Communication— Key to Your Marriage.* It will help you get into the right frame of mind for this chapter

AGREE   DISAGREE

___✓___ ___ 1. Conflict is a part of any human relationship.

___ ___✓___ 2. It is all right to modify the truth to avoid an unpleasant situation.

___ ___✓___ 3. The Christian way to handle your anger at another person's behavior is to keep it inside.

___ ___ 4. When you see a conflict developing between yourself and another person, you should leave or be quiet.

___ ___✓___ 5. It is a sign of spiritual and emotional immaturity for a Christian to be angry.

___ ___✓___ 6. Nothing good ever comes out of conflict.

___ ___✓___ 7. If a person mistreats you, you should solve the problem by avoiding the other person.

___ ___ 8. In a conflict between two people, one of them always loses.

___✓___ ___ 9. Unpleasant feelings (e.g., anger, hate,

jealousy, hurt) toward another person should be expressed to that person.

✓ ____   10. It is possible to express your anger without getting into a fight.

How do you feel about conflict? How do you think other Christians feel about conflict? Would you say that other Christians think conflict is good?

If you think Christians generally think of conflict as bad, you're probably right. For some reason, we've developed the idea that conflict between two people is not Christian. We've developed this opinion in spite of the fact that we see Jesus in conflict throughout the Gospels, and his conflict wasn't only with his religious opponents. He was often in conflict with the disciples, for he seems to have used conflict in a creative way to help the disciples grow in their faith (see, for example, the events surrounding Peter's denial). Yet today most Christians would say conflict is wrong; conflict hurts people; conflict destroys friendships. I must admit that each of those statements is sometimes right, but they aren't always right. In fact, they need never be true if conflict is properly handled.

Although assertiveness training is designed to make all of life smoother, it's particularly helpful in dealing with conflict. As we'll see in this chapter, conflict can be bad—tremendously destructive—but it can also accomplish good things in your life. To be good, conflict needs to be carried on with honesty on your part and respect for the others involved. The tools of assertiveness training give a person a solid foundation for having a good disagreement.

CONFLICT IN THE BIBLE

Let's look briefly at what the Bible has to say about conflict. We'll confine our efforts to one of the most practical books in the Bible, Proverbs. We should also note that conflict in Proverbs is often mentioned under "reproof." Write out in one sentence what these verses say about conflict:

Proverbs 3:11, 12
Proverbs 9:8*b*
Proverbs 12:1

Proverbs 15:10
Proverbs 15:31
Proverbs 17:10
Proverbs 19:25*b*
Proverbs 25:12
Proverbs 27:5
Proverbs 28:23

Although none of these verses condones what we would call fighting, it's clear that rebuking another person or receiving a rebuke from someone is of value. It's a means of growth. But to rebuke another person means conflict. The very heart of rebuke is a difference of opinion serious enough that one person feels called to tell another he is wrong. Rebuke should lead to a conversation about the wrong and attempts to work out a mutually acceptable solution to the difference. But that is conflict. The Bible, then, states as clearly as possible that conflict is good; it has value.

When I was a high schooler and first learning the importance of talking to others about our differences, I gained a good friend by telling him his behavior bothered me. During a meeting one night, as we prayed I knew my attitude toward one of our leaders was not right. I went to him and told him of the difficulty I had with the way he directed our group. He thanked me and asked a few questions to clarify what I meant; then we prayed together. I still consider him a good friend, largely because of the intimacy that developed from our conflict.

Let's examine further Matthew 18:15 as it deals with conflict. This verse makes it plain that when your brother does something that bothers you, you should take up the issue with him. This is proposed by Jesus because failure to do so means you'll eventually lose your brother. (The stated purpose for taking up the conflict is "to gain your brother.") Better to confront him now and resolve the conflict than to let the matter fester until it destroys your friendship.

I would even go so far as to say that if there is no conflict, there is no love. Only love for another person will motivate you sufficiently to go and confront him with the way he has hurt you. Self-interest would simply make you confront him to get your way, but love lets you confront your brother out of concern for growth and development of that relationship.

HIDING DISAGREEMENTS HURTS PEOPLE

Many people think that conflict is bad because they don't realize the consequences of no conflict. If you pretend to agree with another person when in reality you have a strongly different viewpoint, that other person is going to sense your difference through his emotions, even if he can't explain what's happening. That creates anxiety in him at the least, and very often anger. He realizes you aren't being honest, but he doesn't know how to handle it.

Once when I was looking for a job, I worked with the leaders of a denomination I wanted to serve. Unknown to me, the leaders did not want me to serve with their denomination. They never told me that, however. Instead, they pretended to be looking for a place for me by granting my every request for an interview with them. After hours of frustration, I was at last told of their disinterest. I was deeply hurt and quite angry with their deceit. How much better it would have been for everyone had they told me to begin with rather than waste both their time and mine.

Furthermore, if you won't engage in open conflict with another person, you'll often avoid him because being in his presence makes you uncomfortable. It's difficult to be with another person when you have to watch your every word to make certain you avoid conflict. This also causes the other person to be puzzled, sometimes offended. Again, he knows something is wrong but is unable to tell what it is.

The difficulty of watching every word was apparent for me in a ministers' fellowship in my area. The group agreed not to discuss any theology because it was too divisive. That meant you had to watch every word to keep from offending someone. The strain was such that I simply decided it was easier not to attend.

One of the most devastating effects of pretending to agree when in reality you disagree is that somehow your disagreement will surface. Many times it surfaces in little hostile remarks or underhanded digs at the other person. On other occasions it suddenly comes to the surface over a minor, possibly even an unrelated, issue. At that time a person explodes in anger all out of proportion to the incident.

A few years ago I counseled a couple about this very problem. The wife, Alice, never disagreed with her husband no matter how much she inwardly differed with him. Then, after months of silence, she would explode in a rage that shook the household. For days, sometimes even a week or more, no one could talk with her until she would finally settle down into her familiar quietness. Her feigned agreement always led to a time when she would explode because she could no longer contain her feelings.

There are many other consequences of pretending to agree with others when you really don't. On a separate piece of paper list as many as you can think of.

That conflict expresses love is best illustrated by turning to a classic Bible passage on conflict. When Adam and Eve sinned for the first time, their sin was obviously in one sense a difference of opinion with God (Gen. 3). They chose, in an indirect way, to say that they did not agree with him when he told them they could not eat of the tree of the knowledge of good and evil. Rather than facing the issue directly, however, the next time they saw God coming they hid. But God would not allow the conflict to be resolved in that fashion. When they ran and hid, he sought them out. Why? Because he loved them and did not want that conflict to stand between them. He knew it had to be resolved. Because God confronted Adam and Eve about their difference of opinion, it was possible for the relationship, broken through the difference, to be restored. Had God not confronted them about the difference, their relationship could have remained forever broken. This again suggests to us that when something happens that hurts you, that hinders your relationship with another person, you have the responsibility to enter into conflict with that person with the end in view of resolving the conflict and achieving reconciliation.

In fact, I do not think it wrong to say that growth *cannot* come in a human relationship without conflict (conflict here meaning an honest, frank discussion of differences). Unless two people engage periodically in conflict and work through their inevitable differences, they will live in a shallow, surface relationship. When conflicts are being resolved, you learn more about the other person, he learns more about you, and you learn more about yourself. As a result, you grow in your relationship with the other person, discovering things that never would have come to the surface had it not been for the conflict.

A few years ago I was working on a book on divorce. When I finished, my wife began reworking it. Often she came and asked me to explain what I meant in a particular passage. When you have worked hours on a book, attempting to make everything clear, and someone says, "I can't understand this," it's easy to become frustrated, even angry. Yet we worked at it a long time until she understood each detail. Our conflict provided one of the greatest periods of growth in our marriage as we learned more about one another under pressure.

In saying all of this, I'm not saying that conflict is never bad; conflict is frequently bad. But my point here is that conflict properly handled, even as God handled it with Adam and Eve, can be a means of growth in your relationships with others. Conflict does not have to be destructive; it can cause growth.

HOW DO YOU HANDLE CONFLICT?

How do you handle conflict? There are five ways a person can face conflict. As we look at these ways, I want you to determine which type of conflict resolution you use most frequently. Which do you use least frequently? When you get finished, number them from one (most frequent) to five (least frequent) before you continue the chapter.

_____ *I win—you lose.* This is the attitude most people have toward conflict. When two people enter a conflict, one person wins and the other loses. Since losing is never fun, you do everything you can think of to make certain that when the conflict is over, you're the winner. One person gets his way; the other gets nothing. But obviously, if this is the usual form of conflict, one person goes away feeling satisfied and the other leaves feeling defeated. Besides, the defeated one might not graciously accept the defeat. In marriage, this often leads to a covert guerrilla warfare following the decisive battle. The loser takes periodic potshots at the winner while avoiding another full-scale battle. At the same time, if the winner loves the loser, he leaves the conflict with a feeling of guilt because of what he has done.

_____ *Withdrawal.* Some people don't like to lose, so they have figured out a way of avoiding it—they leave the scene of the fight. This obviously means they concede victory to the one who remains on the field of battle, but at least they don't have to face defeat or humiliation in the other person's presence. Again, however, the one who withdraws often continues the fight in subtle ways. The "winner" also leaves with a deep sense of frustration, because he knows the conflict was not resolved.

_____ *Yielding.* In this form of conflict resolution, one person gives in to the other rather than have a conflict. The yielder stays on the field of battle but refuses to fight. This, however, builds resentment over a period of time; it also promotes a lack of respect on the part of the winner toward the yielder. How can you respect someone who won't stand up for his rights?

_____ *Compromise.* There are many people who say this is the best way to resolve conflict. Because it's no fun for anyone to suffer complete defeat and have to surrender in humiliation, let's each experience a little bit of defeat and a little bit of victory. If we do that, we can both walk away satisfied. But this leads to a typical union-management conflict situation. The union greatly inflates its demands so that when the final compromise is worked out, it will have won the greater portion of the pie. At the same time, management is greatly exaggerating its stand so that when the conflict is resolved, *it* will have won the greater portion of the pie. I must admit that compromise of that sort often works, but it can also lead to resentment about what one side did or did not get or about the fairness of the compromise that was worked out. It also works from the premise that the people involved in the conflict are antagonists rather than friends. That may be true in union-management conflicts, but it should not be true in a family or among Christians.

_____ *Mutually agreeable solution.* In this method, a solution is worked out that permits each person to get what he wants. Many people, however, simply don't believe this is possible—but it is. Two people *can* sit down with one another to discuss a difference of opinion, and they *can* honestly discuss what they want out of the situation. They can ask questions and give answers until each has a clear picture of what the other wants. Then they can create a solution that will permit each of them to get all of what he wants. When that happens, it deepens a relationship and promotes harmony. Many times such an approach reveals that the conflict was easily removed when both parties stated what they really wanted out of the situation.

For example, a few days ago two of my sons came to me, asking if we could do something. One wanted to go to a nearby forest preserve, and the other wanted to play baseball. When my third son chimed in with a vote for forest preserve, the other boy burst into tears. He claimed he never got his way, that the other two always voted against him. After a few minutes of thought he said, "Can we bring the baseball equipment to the forest preserve and play there?" The other two thought that was a great idea. Creatively, they proposed a solution that permitted each person to have what he wanted, thus resolving the conflict without anyone's experiencing a loss.

IDEAL CONFLICT

How is it possible for this final, ideal form of conflict to work? Let me describe the method I have developed through working with couples in conflict. First, find the right time and place to settle the conflict. It's very important for two people who have a difference to come together to work it out at a time when both can give their full attention to it. This means that both should be in good health and a good frame of mind. They should be in a place where they will be free from distractions. They should sit facing one another with nothing between them so that they can look into one another's eyes. It's hard to become angry when you are close to a person and looking him right in the eye.

Second, establish a "time out" signal before the conflict begins. By this I mean that the people should establish some signal (such as standing up or raising both hands) that says, "I'm losing control; can we stop for a while and come back to this later?" That way one person doesn't gain an advantage by working on the other's anger or lack of control (such as weeping). The person who calls "time out" suggests a time in the future when they can get together to work on the conflict again until they resolve it. The sooner the time, the better.

Third, it's important for people to begin with a declaration of respect or love and a promise not to attack the other person. That is, one person says to the other something like this: "Although we might really get into it in a few minutes, I want you to know before we start that I'm concerned about solving the problem. I promise not to attack you in any way during this discussion." If that assurance and promise have been given, the conflict can go on in an atmosphere of trust and respect. It lays the groundwork to eliminate all personal comments or name-calling that might destroy the relationship.

Fourth, define the issue. That may sound strange, but so many people get into conflicts without really knowing what they are differing about. This step is so important that the conflict should be defined in writing. When both parties can agree on a written statement describing the conflict, it's certain that the most basic issue will be tackled and not a lot of peripheral issues. This step is so vital that often by the time the issue has been defined, the conflict is resolved. That happens because there was no real conflict, only an apparent one. It dissolved on examination because neither party really knew what the difference was.

Part of point four is to stick to the issue. "Your mother wears combat boots" is a humorous treatment of this statement. You and I laugh when we hear it because we know that many times when couples argue, they argue about one issue and then get sidetracked by a dozen others. Each time a new issue comes up, it should be written down and set aside for future discussion. Only deal with one issue at a time in conflict resolution.

Finally, stick with the problem until both parties are satisfied that it has been resolved. This doesn't mean you have to solve the problem all at one sitting. It doesn't even mean the problem has to be resolved completely in one day. What it means is that you will agree to work together on the problem, even if it takes a month, until both of you are satisfied with the solution you've worked out. It might be necessary to schedule many sessions together until the problem is resolved, but you both agree that you won't quit the discussion until you've established another time when you'll work on it again. A time-out signal is not, then, a means of ducking out of the conflict, but merely a means of heading off a lopsided victory. Time-out means just that—time out until you begin again.

I have found the following conflict resolution sheet, developed by H. Norman Wright, to be very helpful in working out a conflict.

A MODEL FOR RESOLVING CONFLICT

1. Recognize conflict issues—don't ignore them.
2. Listen carefully to the other person (Prov. 18:13).
3. Select an appropriate time for settling the conflict.
4. Specifically define the conflict.
   a. How do you define the conflict?
   b. How do you think the other person defines the conflict?
   c. What behaviors contribute to the conflict, in your opinion?
   d. What behaviors do you think the other person sees as contributing to the conflict?
   e. What are the issues of agreement? of disagreement?
5. Identify your own contribution to the problem.
   a. Choose one word to describe what you want to discuss.
   b. State the word or subject in one complete sentence. Be precise and specific.
6. Identify several alternate solutions.
7. Decide on a mutually acceptable solution.
   a. What steps must you take in order to implement this solution?
   b. What are the possible outcomes of implementing this solution?
8. Implement the new behaviors.

Assignment: Work out a conflict with a friend or relative. (If you're married, your spouse is a good person to work with, abiding by the rules of this chapter.)

Keep a record during the week of the different times you use each of the different conflict resolution styles. Does your record reveal that you really use the styles in the way you numbered them in this chapter, or does the record reveal a different pattern from what you wrote down?

SIX
Sending I-messages

What should you do when someone hurts you? "Grin and bear it"? No, when someone hurts you, you should express your hurt and also a desire for reconciliation. But unless you use the tools of assertiveness (which we will look at in the next two chapters) you might create more hurt by your attempted reconciliation than existed before you began to talk.

There are a number of reasons why you should express your hurt and seek reconciliation. First, Ephesians 4:25 says that you should speak the truth in love. By not revealing the hurt you experience with your friend, you prevent him from achieving reconciliation with you. Further, Matthew 18:15 says that when someone hurts you, you have a responsibility to go to that person and express your feelings with the intention of seeking reconciliation. This is all based on the character of God as demonstrated in Genesis 3. There God expresses his hurt over Adam's and Eve's sin by seeking them out for reconciliation. Because God cared for Adam and Eve, he sought reconciliation; therefore, love is also demonstrated in your life when you seek reconciliation by making known your hurt to those who offend you.

However, there is another side to this matter. If you fail to communicate when someone hurts you, you are being judgmental. You are saying to yourself, "He couldn't handle this information if I did tell him." You think that he might lose control of himself in rage, that he might reject you as a friend, that he might become upset because he hadn't intended to hurt you. There are many different judgments you make against a person when you fail to speak about your hurts. List some of the other judgments you make when you refuse to let a person know about your hurt.

Express your hurt—that's what is needed. But there are many people who express their hurt in such a way that they create further conflict rather than resolving the conflict that already exists. They do this by sending what I call "you-messages" rather than "I-messages."

I-MESSAGES

Communication in the midst of a conflict should be carefully thought out, using well-chosen words. One aspect of this is what marriage and family specialists have come to call sending "I-messages." In this positive communication, a person attempts to express his feelings about a situation for the purpose of solving the problem without *unnecessarily* offending.

Note that we are talking about feelings in this situation. Although feelings dominate current discussion about family living to too great an extent, we cannot deny that feelings play a major role in interpersonal relationships. In most instances, feelings about what has happened are the major problem. As we saw in the last chapter, everyone reacts differently to a given situation. My response and yours will be different. If yours is negative, or if you feel hurt as a result of what has happened, you have a responsibility to make known that hurt. However, an important qualification needs to be made: you must assume responsibility for your feelings. You cannot blame the other person for how you feel, no matter what happened.

I-messages express your feelings about what happened. For instance, let's say that in the midst of a conversation with me, you suddenly turn and walk away to talk with someone else. I feel hurt when that happens. (Another person might say inwardly, *I know he has something important to say to Susan, so I'll wait until he returns,* without ever feeling any hurt.) When I have occasion to talk again with you, I should tell you that I felt hurt when you walked away. By focusing on my feelings, I avoid judging you or blaming you as I would by saying, "You hurt me when you walked away." That's not true. The truth of the matter is that I *felt* hurt—that is the problem we need to deal with.

Let's look at four characteristics of I-messages. First, I-messages tell other people how you feel or think. As we have noted, this means you are concentrating on what is going on inside you. It also means that you are not laying blame on anyone else for the way you feel. You alone are responsible for your feelings. No one else can determine how you will feel by his behavior.

Let's pause for a moment here and examine a statement I often make: "How you feel about a situation is far more important than what actually happened." *Is that really the case?* Yes. Your feelings are a result of what you tell yourself about what happened.

If you have an accident with the car, you can tell yourself many different things. You can tell yourself, *You sure are a miserable driver to get yourself into this mess.* Obviously, that will make you feel bad. You can also tell yourself, *Under these driving conditions, I guess accidents like this are almost inevitable. I'd better get done with the job of notifying the authorities and keeping others from becoming involved in another accident.* That should permit you to calm down quite rapidly, because it is a blame-free message. You can go even further and tell yourself, *God must have something in mind that he wants to accomplish through this. I wonder what it will be?* By speaking like that, you create a feeling of expectation. In each instance, however, your inner conversation with yourself is the key to your feelings.

Thought, even though it might be unconscious, always precedes feelings; feelings never create thought. Thus we return to our original idea that how you feel about a situation is far more important than what actually happened. This means that when I say that the problems leading to conflict between people are their feelings rather than their actions, I am simply amplifying this idea. There is a counterthought for every negative feeling, one that will turn bad feeling into good if only you will put forth the effort to find it.

Second, I-messages make you vulnerable. When you express directly to another person your own ideas or feelings, you expose yourself to criticism or ridicule. If you say, "When you walked away to talk with Susan in the midst of our conversation, I felt hurt," your friend can respond, "That was dumb. I just had to talk to her. You should have known I'd be back to talk with you in a few minutes." This is why many people ask indirect questions or refuse to tell others how they feel or what they think or want. They're afraid that someone will reject what they say, and they would rather be quiet than take that risk. Because we learn this lesson early in life, changing it often requires the help of a loving friend.

But vulnerability and honesty are two sides of the same coin. As soon as you're honest with people about what you think, feel, or want, you're also vulnerable. You can't have one without the other. At the same time, it's impossible to have deep relationships with others unless you're willing to be honest—and, therefore, vulnerable.

Third, I-messages communicate to others a less threatening or even a nonthreatening message because they involve your feelings, your opinions, or your wants rather than the other person's actions. Let me illustrate.

Which of these statements would promote an open exchange of opinions leading to resolution of a problem? (1) "You really hurt me when you left to talk with Susan. I sometimes think you get pleasure out of hurting others." (2) "I felt hurt when you went to talk with Susan in the midst of our conversation. I sometimes feel as if you think nothing of my feelings."

Both of these statements are obviously going to result in conflict, but the second expresses feelings that might lead to a good discussion to solve the problem at hand. The first is an attack. It blames the other person immediately, when in reality he may have been completely ignorant of the effect of his behavior. Thus we see the importance of using I-messages in communication. They communicate a message with as low a threat potential as possible.

Finally, I-messages are attempts on your part to deal with the actual problem—your feelings—rather than an attempt to focus attention elsewhere. If you focus on your feelings, you reduce the threat to the other person to the lowest possible level. Furthermore, you direct his attention to the problem you need to handle. You don't pretend that the problem is him or anything he is doing; rather, the problem is the way you react to what he does.

If you make known your feelings in this manner, he can join you in a search for some way to solve the problem.

At the conclusion of our discussion of I-messages we need to face a very real problem. We've been assuming that the differences you have with others are not moral issues—and most are not. But let's suppose you do face a very real moral issue. For instance, consider this hypothetical situation: A Christian friend, Phil, lied about you, telling people in the church that you used church money to buy a new sofa for your home. Can you handle this with principles derived from assertiveness training? Is the problem now just a matter of your feelings, or is it a matter of sin that must be corrected?

In many ways a clear-cut sin will be treated differently, yet not entirely so. In dealing with actual sin, I have found that speaking in a straightforward manner has often had negative effects. Saying to Phil, "Brother, you sinned against me when you told those lies about where I got the money for my new sofa," will cause Phil to become defensive, possibly even hostile. But if you say (using I-messages), "Phil, I was really hurt when Ray told me you were telling people I paid for my new sofa with church money, " you bring the sin into the open. At the same time the second statement will sufficiently defuse the tension to permit Phil to respond both to my hurt and to his own sin. As a secondary benefit, it permits him to disclaim involvement in the sin if your information was wrong.

Thus, while a situation involving sin is obviously very serious (I think I would pray far more if sin were involved than if only I had been hurt), the basic tools of assertiveness will still provide an effective way of handling the situation.

YOU-MESSAGES

The opposite of I-messages are what I call you-messages. Let's look at four characteristics of you-messages that create problems in interpersonal relationships.

First, you-messages are judgments you make about other people. When you say "You hurt me," you immediately express a judgment about the other person. Frequently associated with this in the other person's mind is the idea, *And you think I did it on purpose!* But to say that another person hurt you (speaking of your emotions) is to say that you are not responsible for your feelings. Others are. That denies the basic teaching of the Bible that you will be judged for the way you act and react. *You* are responsible for your own emotions and behavior. Another person cannot determine how you'll feel. Only you can decide that. It's *your thoughts* about what happened that make you feel hurt, not the other person's behavior.

For example, if the friend who broke off your conversation to talk to Susan were a three year old, you wouldn't feel hurt. You'd immediately think, *What else can you expect from a child?* Or if you knew Susan had a very serious problem that your friend could solve, but that she always left immediately after the meeting you attended because she had to be to work ten minutes later, you might think, *I appreciate Aaron's concern for Susan. He'll be back in just a minute, and then we can finish our conversation.* These illustrations show again that what really counts is not so much what happens, but your thoughts about what happens.

Second, you-messages are judgmental because they avoid the real problem—your feelings—and focus on a secondary problem—the other person's behavior or attitudes.

Third, because you-messages are judgmental (and are viewed that way by the other person), they are threatening to the recipient. If you say, "You hurt me," you're attacking the other person. If you say, "I felt hurt when you . . .," you focus attention on your feelings, posing only a relatively minor threat to the other person. The reason for using I-messages is to minimize the threat involved, to create a climate in which you can discuss your problem and reach a mutually agreeable solution without anger or resentment. If you begin by attacking the other person with a judgment about his behavior, the possibility of an anger-free environment in which you can focus on the problem and resolve it is slight.

Finally, you-messages are self-serving, protective devices. They protect you by attacking the other person; they protect you by making judgments about the other person, drawing attention away from your feelings. They hide your inner feelings from exposure. Such hiding will do nothing to resolve your conflict with the other person, but will in all likelihood intensify it.

I-messages, then, are more Christian than you-messages for a number of reasons. They truthfully face the problem between you and another person—your feelings about what happened. They face the real problem rather than a false one; they are self-revealing, thus creating an atmosphere in which others can express their feelings and you can grow together. They avoid manipulation by permitting the other person to face the real problem rather than your attempts to get your way without revealing what you really want.

All of this leads us back to the Bible verses we used at the beginning of this chapter. Ephesians 4:25 says that you should speak the truth always with your neighbor. That is only possible with I-messages rather than the more common you-messages. I-messages also seem more fitting as a means of following Jesus' instruction to speak *in the hope of achieving reconciliation* to your brother who offends you. That cannot be accomplished effectively if you use you-messages. Finally, I-messages demonstrate the same sort of confronting love that God revealed in the Garden of Eden when he spoke with Adam and Eve about their sin; it's love that won't let hurt feelings remain, but will openly confront those feelings, with the knowledge that reconciliation occurs no other way.

Now, having said all this about I-messages, let me give a pattern for sending an I-message. You send I-messages when you say something like this: "I feel [name an emotion] when [describe the event that you reacted to]." On the other hand, you-messages generally begin with the word "you" and cast blame on the other person. Care needs to be exercised when sending I-messages that you don't begin by saying, "I feel [name an emotion]," and then cast blame on the other person. It is not simply the form that concerns us, but the accompanying attitude that you are responsible for your own feelings.

Assignment: (1) Analyze the following statements to determine whether they are I-messages or you-messages. The key follows. If you get more than five wrong, you should reread this chapter, so that you may better understand it.

"I"   "YOU"

_____ _____   1. I feel picked on when you criticize my work.

_____ _____   2. I feel like a fool because you criticize most of the work I do around the house.

_____ _____   3. I'm frustrated. I feel that most of the things I do around the house are not appreciated.

_____ _____   4. I feel depressed when I plan dinner for both of us and you call at the last minute, saying you have to work.

_____ _____   5. I am depressed because you called at the last minute to tell me you wouldn't be home for dinner.

_____ _____   6. You make me depressed when you call at the last minute and tell me you can't make it home for dinner.

_____ _____   7. I feel that you're unfair when you criticize me in public.

_____ _____   8. I feel hurt when I am criticized in front of other people.

_____ _____   9. You hurt me tonight when you told Joann that I can't cook a steak half as well as she does.

_____ _____   10. You hurt me when you make fun of my relatives.

_____ _____   11. I was hurt today when you made fun of my relatives.

_____ _____   12. I feel hurt when someone makes fun of my relatives.

_____ _____   13. When you criticize the way I keep house, I feel useless.

_____ _____   14. Why do you criticize the way I keep house when you know that hurts me?

____	____	15. I feel useless when you criticize the way I keep house.
____	____	16. I feel rebellious when I am nagged about doing work on the house.
____	____	17. You make me rebel when you nag me about doing work on the house.
____	____	18. When you nag me about doing work around the house, I rebel.
____	____	19. I feel as if I am being attacked when you want to talk immediately after I get home about everything I did today at work.
____	____	20. I feel like you attack me when you want to talk immediately after I get home about everything I did today at work.
____	____	21. Give me a minute to rest when I get home before you begin asking questions about what I did at work during the day.

Answer Key:

I-messages: 1, 3, 4, 8, 11 (poor because it blames the other person), 12, 15, 16 (poor because it attacks with "nag"), 19.
You-messages: 2, 5, 6, 7, 9, 10, 13, 14, 17, 18, 20.
Neither: 21.

(2) This week, keep track of your feelings about things others do. Practice using I-messages to express your feelings. Note the difference when you fail and use a you-message.

SEVEN
Active Listening

"God gave us one mouth and two ears; we do well to use them in that proportion." However, we all know that few people follow that guideline, and there are many who reverse it. Listening, nonetheless, is far more important than talking. Not the least reason is that when you listen you're learning, but when you're talking you're simply repeating what you already know—or think you know.

Strange as it may seem to many people, listening is probably as important as talking in assertive behavior. Although assertiveness means expressing your feelings, thoughts, and opinions, it also includes respect for others. What demonstrates more effectively your respect for another human being than paying close attention as he talks? What demonstrates respect less than ignoring his remarks for something you consider more important?

Biblical principles should dominate your thinking about listening. Let's look briefly at what the Bible has to say about it. Write out in one sentence the teaching on listening given in each of the following verses: Proverbs 18:13; 21:28; James 1:19, 20.

Listening is more important than speaking, as we have already noted. But you should also recognize that if you listen well, others will listen when you speak. If you will not listen as they speak, they will soon learn to ignore what you say when you speak. Finally, we should note that it's foolish to speak with another person about anything when you haven't first heard him out. You simply cannot know what you are talking about if you haven't first listened.

COMMUNICATION PROBLEMS

In contrast to those principles, most people spend the time while others are talking in thinking about what they are going to say next. As soon as the speaker is finished, the next person jumps into the conversation, never pausing to consider what has been said. That results in needless confusion.

Norman Wright points out that there are six steps in the communication process and that misunderstandings can arise at any point after the first. When you prepare to speak, you start with an idea in your head. That is what you want to communicate to others.

Second, you put that idea into words. But the words are always an imperfect expression of what you originally meant to say. They convey to the other person a less-than-perfect expression of your idea.

Third, the other person hears the words you have spoken. Because they are already an imperfect expression of the idea you wanted to convey, it's easy to see where misunderstanding might occur.

Fourth, the other person hears your words against the background of his own thought. As a result, he receives an impression of what *he thought* you said. Since your original idea was imperfectly expressed by your words, his imperfect hearing of those words opens further possibilities for misunderstanding.

Next, we have the person's own expression of what he thought you said. Inasmuch as he also found it necessary to take an idea in his mind and translate that into words for you, there is yet another opportunity for misunderstanding.

Finally, we are left with what you think the other person said about what you originally said. The following summarizes the six steps:

1. You have the original idea.
2. Your idea is put into words.

3. Your words are heard by the listener.
4. Your listener interprets your words.
5. Your listener seeks to express by his own words your idea translated into his idea of what you said.
6. You hear his words.

As one regularly engaged in communication as a profession, I assume that at least half the time I fail to communicate effectively. This also applies in everyday conversation, including the very special conversation that occurs between husband and wife. By assuming that I fail at least half the time, I have a much greater opportunity to correct my failures by second attempts.

Have you ever played the game "Rumor"? If you have, the preceding discussion had added meaning for you. "Rumor" is a game in which everyone sits in a circle. One person begins by whispering a story to the person sitting to his right. That person tells the story to the person on his right. When the story at last gets to the final person, he tells the story to the whole group. That is followed by the first person's reciting the original story. The difference between the two stories is often astonishing. Even when we want to, we find it very difficult to repeat a story that another person has given us.

The solution to this is a communication tool called "active listening."

What is active listening? In active listening, you respond to the speaker by attempting to feed back to him what you think his feelings or thoughts were. That gives the speaker an opportunity to verify the accuracy of your interpretation. The style to use goes something like this: "This is what I heard you say. [You then repeat what you heard in your own words.] Did I understand you?" The other person can then respond in one of two ways: "Yes, completely," or, "You only partially understood me. Let me repeat it." He then repeats his statement, giving particular emphasis to the portion you didn't understand. You then repeat the process until at last the speaker is able to say, "Yes, completely."

When people hear this for the first time, many laugh. "You really don't mean that you actually talk like that, do you?" they ask. "Talking like that must take a lot of time." Yes, I actually talk like that in a conflict, and even at other times.

Yes, talking like that takes a lot of time, but it's worth it in terms of the value I place on my relationships with others.

Active listening has an important purpose behind it. The basic motive for active listening is love. If you really love other people, you want to listen with as much care as possible. You don't want to hear only the words they speak, but also the emotions that underlie those words.

Communication is a multifaceted event. You communicate with the words you speak, but you also communicate with the tone of your voice, the volume you use, the expression on your face, the position of your body, and many more items so subtle that you never notice them unless you're studying others as they communicate.

When you listen, then, you must hear far more than words. You need to hear the speaker's tone and volume, and you also need to "hear" his facial expressions and his body language. This means that when he is finished speaking, your response is far more than repeating his words. You reflect what he wanted to communicate through all the elements in communication.

As you see the highly complex nature of communication, you can see the importance of active listening. And if active listening is important under normal circumstances, when you're engaged in conversation involving little emotion, how much more important is it when you're carrying on a conversation charged with emotion, as in a conflict?

RIGHT ATTITUDES

Active listening requires attitudes on your part that grow out of love for others. First, you must really *want* to hear what the other person has to say. That means you're willing to take the time to listen or to state that you cannot listen right at that time. Wanting to hear what the other person has to say—that's the catch. In many instances you, like all people, are so oriented toward your own needs that you aren't willing to listen to what the other person has to say. It may be that you think you know ahead of time what will be said. (Proverbs says that the man who thinks this is a fool.) It may be that your own needs are so desperate that you can't really listen to another person. In any case, when you won't or can't listen to another person, love demands that you tell him so. Love also demands that you set a time in the near future when you will be willing and able to talk.

Wanting to hear what another person has to say takes discipline. That is particularly true in a family. I find that many times it's necessary to lay aside a book and say, "I'm sorry, I wasn't really listening. Would you please repeat what you said now that I can give you my full attention?" It might mean turning off the television, laying down some tools, or stopping your preparation for dinner. Wanting to hear what another person has to say means stopping whatever else you're doing and giving that person your full attention. If you are unwilling to do that, you should admit it so that the other person won't waste time attempting to communicate with you.

A situation in which a husband refuses to pay attention to or listen to his wife brings about "nagging." What happens is that the wife begins to talk to her husband, but as she talks, she realizes he isn't listening. That frustrates her, causing her to talk more or louder in the hope of breaking through his disinterest. If only he would give her his full attention, she would stop nagging. (The first time she would probably faint.)

Second, in active listening you must genuinely want to help the other person with his problem. This is obviously closely related to the first attitude required for active listening, but it's something more. Unless you really want to help the person who is talking to you, you won't give him your attention. Your mind will wander. When the time comes to discuss possible solutions, you'll give less than your best. Again, love demands that if you're unwilling to help the other person, you should honestly admit that and give the person a chance to seek counsel elsewhere.

Third, you must be willing and able to accept any feelings the other person reveals, no matter how different from your own or how foolish you might think they are. That is a big order. There are certain feelings that you have a hard time accepting in other people because of your background. Anger is difficult for me to accept. But if you are going to listen with any effect, you have to be able to accept any feeling or desire the other person expresses. This doesn't mean, of course, that you condone the feelings; it doesn't mean you'll go along with the ideas the person has as a result of his feelings. It simply means that you can accept what the other person says as a correct interpretation of how he feels at the moment. Just because the emotions are very different from what you would experience in the same situation doesn't mean you have to reject them. Each of us experiences events in different ways. If you're to listen effectively, you need to develop the ability to accept any emotion the other person might have.

Recently a friend revealed to me considerable anger about an event he experienced. As I looked at the problem, I could see many ways to respond other than in anger. But *his* emotion was anger. I listened carefully, saying that I could understand his feeling. The only way I could help was by putting myself into his place and accepting his emotions of the moment.

Fourth, you have to be willing to trust the other person to work out his problems without your advice. At this point you, like myself and many others, may have difficulties. You may have something bordering on a messiah complex when another person reveals a problem from his life. You think that what he needs more than anything else is your wisdom. As a result, you listen, then jump in with a solution the moment he's finished. You fail to realize (we all do) that most people can solve their own problems if given a chance. Active listening helps the person talk through his problem and clarify what is bothering him. As a result, you serve a valuable function by listening. You enable the other person to so clarify his thinking that he can fashion a good solution without any assistance. Love trusts the other person to create a solution to the problem.

During high school and college, I spent considerable time with Bill Gothard. I would often discuss with him a problem that concerned me. As I talked, he practiced active listening. On many occasions, by the time I was finished talking, I could lay out my proposed solution, yet he had told me nothing about what I should do. His listening helped me clarify my problem sufficiently so that I could solve it on my own.

Fifth, you need to learn to appreciate the fact that feelings are often temporary and frequently need only the release of conversation. Everyone at some time or another has an experience so frustrating that he simply must talk with someone about it. A person comes in at full steam and blasts away about whatever happened. An hour later he wonders what it was that got him so upset. You need to learn that others are the same way. Give someone a chance to express the feelings that come from an experience and the emotion will frequently dissipate. All the person needs is a listening ear. As a result, emotions that you would find unacceptable if they continued, disappear as a result of being expressed.

How often I have seen this with my children. One of them gets hurt while playing. He comes into the house, all upset about what has happened. He expresses some strong emotions about his hurt. When he is finished I say, "Is it all right now?" Almost invariably he responds, "Yep," and is gone back to his playing. Adults are often the same. If only someone will hear them out about their hurt, they'll be fine in a while.

Finally, and this is the key to all other attitudes, you need to learn how to view the other person as different from yourself. That person you are listening to has different emotions and a different identity from your own. This attitude is probably more difficult for parents than for anyone else. They have a difficult time seeing that their children are different from them. The children have a right to act differently, have different emotions from their parents, and hold different ideas. Nonetheless, it is only as parents permit their children to be different from themselves that they can ever have a good relationship with them.

When each of us comes to the point that he can accept others as very different from himself, he can begin to listen effectively to what they have to say.

A CASE IN POINT

Let's take this theoretical discussion of active listening and apply it to a particular case. Let's assume that your neighbor rings your doorbell. When you open the door, he immediately begins to speak rapidly and loudly, demonstrating great anger about something you apparently did. How should you handle this using the principles we developed in the last two chapters? Write out your answer.

Now here is my suggestion. Begin using active listening by stating, "If I hear you right, you're really angry. Am I right in thinking you're angry because I let my guests park in front of your house last night, and one of them stepped on a newly planted rose bush?"

After listening to his answer you can again respond, "I can see this really has you upset. If I hear you right, you're also saying you think I should pay to have your rose plant replaced?"

Again, you're granting him the right to his emotion while seeking to clarify or understand just what he wants. At this point you may have a problem. You feel no responsibility for your guest's action. Even in the face of his anger you state, "Even though I sympathize with your feelings, I don't think I'm responsible for my guest's mistake. Could I call my guest and tell him what happened, explaining your feelings to him?"

You recognize again the validity of his feelings, which is very important when emotions are high. But using an I-message, you express your own thought. While he might differ, you haven't complicated matters further by accusing him of treating you wrongly by his demand for payment.

What happens if he continues to demand payment, unwilling to accept your offer to speak with your guest? You repeat your statement about not paying but being willing to help. If he continues to be abusive, you can quietly state, "While I recognize your right to your opinion, unless you recognize my refusal to pay but willingness to help, I'll simply close my door."

You're polite but firm. You've done everything you can. No one can guarantee that every problem can be solved easily just because you use the methods of assertiveness training. Some people are downright hard to get along with. Others are totally unreasonable. None of that is an excuse for you to become either aggressive or passive. Unless someone actually becomes physically violent, you always have the option of stating plainly that you will not talk anymore—and then leaving.

My concern is that you see that assertive behavior will work no matter what situation you face. In most instances, active listening combined with I-messages will defuse major emotions. Even if you can't complete your conversation at the time, by respecting the other person's rights, you usually lay the groundwork for a future, fruitful conversation. That isn't always easy. Sometimes you'll lose control, too. But as you learn how to use the tools given in this book, you'll be able to handle better any situation you face. And you'll do it with far less trouble than you ever have in the past.

Assignment: At the heart of active listening is the ability to ask good questions. This exercise is designed to develop that ability. Once each day during the coming week, carry on a conversation with someone doing nothing more than asking questions. Never make a statement reflecting your own feelings or thoughts. Just ask questions.

EIGHT
Anger: Good? Bad? Indifferent?

"If you don't get angry occasionally, something is seriously wrong with you, for anger is a perfectly normal human emotion."

For many Christians, this statement causes problems. For some reason, many of us picked up the idea that anger, all anger, is wrong. This may be because our parents disciplined us for any expression of anger. It may also come from the fact that our school teachers didn't let us express anger. Whatever the reason, a good many people think that any anger is wrong. Not so!

Anger is a natural response to many situations. You experience anger when people important to you reject you—even sometimes when people unimportant to you reject you. You experience anger in the face of humiliation. You also experience anger in the face of frustration. The common element is that your rights (real or imagined) have been violated. We aren't talking at this point only about the rights in the bill of rights discussed earlier, but about many of the rights we feel we have as human beings.

There are other instances when you get angry. You usually experience anger when you see a wrong committed. The Bible frequently speaks about the rights of the poor, the need for justice, and the need for righteousness. When you see clear violations of those basic principles, you get angry. You don't think it's right for people to experience the extremes of poverty you often see depicted on the evening news. You don't think it's right for the rich to escape punishment because they can tie up the courts through extensive appeals while the average person suffers the full weight of the law. You don't think it's right when cheaters get wealthy and assume positions of power as a result of their sinful activity. You get angry when those things happen. Anger appears to be not only the usual human response to those situations, but also the most natural response.

BIBLICAL TEACHING ON ANGER

But none of this faces the question, "Is anger right or is anger always wrong?" Again, let's examine what the Bible has to say on the subject. Write out a one-sentence summary of each of the following verses, explaining what it teaches about anger.

Proverbs 15:1
Proverbs 15:18
Proverbs 16:32
Proverbs 19:11
Proverbs 20:2
Proverbs 22:24, 25
Proverbs 29:11
Proverbs 29:22
Mark 3:5
Ephesians 4:26
Ephesians 4:31
Colossians 3:8
Colossians 3:21
James 1:19, 20

Now examine the sentences to determine what you learned. Are there any common themes running through these verses? You should find some.

In the New Testament there are three Greek words for "anger." Each gives us a different perspective. The first word is *thumas.* We use the word "explode" when we speak of this kind of anger. It comes suddenly and with tremendous fury, just like a thunderstorm. But it's also quickly gone. The

Greeks often spoke of this as the beginning of anger. If it didn't disappear quickly it would become a sustained anger, but usually it's just an explosion that is soon gone, leaving destruction in its wake. Galatians 5:20 and Ephesians 4:31 describe this kind of anger.

A second word, *parorgismos,* describes anger that has been provoked. This anger leads to continuing irritation. It contains the feelings of revenge and exasperation at another. The Bible uses this only three times, and never in a good sense (Rom. 10:19; Eph. 4:26*b*; 6:4). It is interesting that this word and its use recognize that another person should not be able to provoke you to anger. You should have control of your emotional response to another's activity. You are responsible for the way you behave. Revenge and bitterness against another have no place in your life.

The final and most common word for anger is *orge.* This word refers to a more settled, enduring form of anger. It's the word used most frequently to describe God's attitude toward sin. He's against it, so strongly against it that he's angry that it takes place and angry with those who do it. Because we are made in the image of God, it follows logically that the emotions he experiences we may also experience without sin. Thus, although *orge* anger can be wrong, it can also be right. We can be justly angry, even as God is angry but does not sin.

As you look at the biblical teaching on anger, a number of points stand out. First, anger is frequently wrong. Particularly is this the case if you nurse it along after the first flash of heat. Ephesians 4:26 speaks about this when it says, "Do not let the sun go down on your anger." But if you examine all the references to anger, you discover that more often than not the Bible talks about the wrong of being angry. In most instances, anger is wrong. You sin more often than not when you are angry. You get angry for the wrong reasons. You get angry at the wrong people or things, you get excessively angry about things; you remain angry too long; and you don't forgive soon enough. Most of the time, when you get angry you sin.

Probably where you, like me, fail most often is in nursing your anger. You cannot be angry and then drop it. You feel the need to nurse the anger along, thinking of things that should have happened, that could happen in the future, thinking of means of revenge. In all of this you cultivate a spirit of bitterness, irritation, or revenge. When you do that you are wrong, you are sinning.

Nursed anger is wrong primarily because of what it does to others. First of all, it is unloving. It demonstrates that you are not forgiving the one at whom you're angry. That hurts those who wronged you, and it sometimes hurts others nearby who didn't wrong you but observed what happened. Nursed anger makes normal relations with anyone difficult, because it stifles the emotion of love that is necessary to maintaining normal relations. It focuses your attention so strongly on the source of your anger that you are unable to see others' needs and meet them.

More than anything else, however, anger is selfish. It's a demand you make on other people to conform to your expectations for their behavior. When they fail, you become angry with them. While you might not realize it, because you learned the behavior so early in life, your anger is often a means of forcing others to conform to your expectations. They soon learn that if they fail to conform, they'll experience your wrath. Because few people are willing to confront an angry person, they conform. As I stated in the first chapter, that is manipulation. We want to give up all forms of manipulation in order to speak the truth in love. Thus you must renounce anger as a method of dealing with other people, as a method of making them conform to your expectations.

WHEN ANGER IS GOOD

However, I don't want you to get the impression that anger is always wrong. That would be as unbiblical as thinking that anger is always right. I would even go so far as to suggest that the inability to get angry is wrong. If you can see a little child injured deliberately by an adult without reacting in anger, something is wrong. If you can see people suffering extreme poverty as a result of political oppression and not become angry, something is wrong. If you can see unjust men rise to power through unrighteous means and not get angry, something is wrong. God gets angry at sin, and you should also. If you can't get angry when you see sin, you have lost the ability to have compassion, and that's a serious matter. You need to cultivate again a biblical attitude toward wrong that permits you to get angry.

Few people have trouble getting angry, but those who do face a long, hard struggle to regain the ability to become angry. I'll never forget a woman I counseled who had lost the ability to get angry. Her husband could do anything he wanted and she would remain unflappable. Even as I checked with her in private, I saw the same attitude. I tried to upset her myself to see if somehow I could provoke her to anger. It was impossible. Eventually, counseling broke down because she did not see her inability as a problem, even though it was tearing her marriage apart. Because she would not get upset at anything, she had no motivation to correct the problems destroying her marriage. If they upset her husband, that was his problem. She had her life and was enjoying it. She wouldn't let him do anything that would upset her; she could not get angry, so she also had no motivation to work at solving her problems.

Thus, we see that anger can be good. The Bible is careful as it talks about good anger. It says you should be slow to get angry (James 1:19, 20). It doesn't encourage explosive outbursts that come and go very rapidly and leave little other than destruction in their wake. It doesn't encourage anger in which vengeance is a strong part of the emotion. But the Bible does suggest that you need to get angry—even if it is slowly.

Why do you need to get angry? Because if you cannot get angry, you'll never be sufficiently motivated to right some of the wrongs you see around you or that you experience yourself.

As I went through college and seminary, I prepared myself for a ministry of marriage and family education. I wanted to be involved with a ministry that would strengthen marriages and families so that Christians could devote the energy often lost there to other tasks. That conviction was largely an intellectual one because I had little contact with people in counseling settings.

Then I had a couple come in to talk with me. They were a classic case. Both grew up in Christian homes and graduated from a well-known college. They were married by the college chaplain late in their senior year. Now they were talking with me about a problem that was literally pulling their marriage apart. He wanted to live in one part of the country and she wanted to live in another. Neither was willing to give an inch.

As I spoke with them, I discovered that major problems had existed in their marriage from the start. They wanted no more counseling than one session, and they only accepted that to satisfy their parents.

After they left my office, I went home with a burning anger at the attitude toward marriage in the churches. We give people no preparation to speak of and we give them little or no support afterward, but we thoroughly condemn them if they have problems they can't solve. I determined then to do everything I could to see that couples were properly prepared for marriage in every church I would ever be associated with, and I also resolved that they would have the best support we could give during the first years of their marriage as they were establishing the patterns they would live by. My anger remains. It continues to motivate me to work with people in marriage preparation and marriage enrichment. I can't forget my deepseated response to that problem. My anger is what motivates me to work toward solving this problem wherever I have any influence.

Anger is also the motivating force in helping you clear up differences with other people. Because anger creates an unsettled state inside you, it motivates you to clear up your differences. As with the woman who lost the ability to be angry and then couldn't work on the problems in her marriage because they didn't bother her, so if you lose the ability to get angry, you also lack the motivation to clear up differences with others. Your anger gets you moving; it motivates you to solve the problem because you don't like the feelings associated with anger.

HOW DO YOU HANDLE ANGER?

This brings us to the point of asking, "How do you handle anger?" There are four ways people handle anger. Which do you use most frequently? Many people *repress* anger. That means they never really admit they're angry. Unconsciously they're pushing the anger down inside themselves where it can't be found.

A few years ago one of the women in my church told me she was having a problem with anger. The senior minister gave her a book dealing with the subject. She asked him, "Is this a Christian book?" Instead of answering her question he said, "The book was written by a minister." However, he and I both knew that the minister's viewpoint was far from being Christian. A few days later, Ruthann (not her real name) fell into conversation with me about anger. When I mentioned the book we use for anger (not knowing the senior pastor had already given it to her) I said, "Why don't you read this book? It's not really from a Christian perspective, but it has some good principles that in no way contradict the Bible."

Her anger immediately surfaced. "Not a Christian book? What do you mean? Pastor told me it was a Christian book. Why don't you think it's Christian?" I begged off contradicting my colleague until I could speak with him further. I pointed out, however, that Ruthann was now experiencing considerable anger. She vehemently denied it. She told me, almost in a shout, "I'm not angry!" She very effectively repressed her anger. She did such a fine job that she didn't know she was angry, even though anyone else present would have quickly sensed it.

Repression, however, has its price. Ruthann was subject to frequent attacks of acid stomach; she often got severe migraine headaches; she was highly nervous. All of those come from repressing anger. It doesn't work. Whatever emotion you deny will catch up with you in some way; it needs to get out, and it will. You determine whether it will come out in healthy ways or whether it will slowly undermine your health. Either way, though, it will come out no matter what you do.

A second way of handling anger is through *suppression*. Many people think of suppression and repression as the same, but they aren't. Repression is unconscious. When anger arises you don't even acknowledge it; often you aren't even aware that you're angry; but your unconscious defense mechanisms force the anger into your subconscious, where it will not consciously disturb you. On the other hand, suppression is a conscious activity. You know you're angry, but you choose not to express your anger because of what you view as the consequences. As a result, you consciously push the anger aside, knowing you'll have to deal with it face-to-face at some time in the future.

We obviously consider suppression in certain situations. When your boss comes in very upset about something and humiliates you in front of the whole office, you can't help but get angry. But what happens if you express your anger right back at him? There's a good chance you'll be fired, so you suppress it. You say nothing, planning to deal with the anger at some future time when the atmosphere is more conducive to a solution. (You can talk to him or, if that won't work, to someone else who can listen and understand your feelings.)

Or you are suddenly confronted by a huge man as you walk home late at night. He stands in front of you and demands that you give him your wallet. Along with his demands he makes some snide remarks about your appearance, almost as if looking for a fight. Now, you might be angry; but unless you have special skills in fighting, you'll surrender your wallet without a word. You suppress your anger because you know that expressing it might be fatal.

Suppression, because it's a conscious way of handling anger, is good—so long as it's not the only way you handle anger. It can also be bad if used too often or in inappropriate situations. Suppression properly used means that you will consciously deal with your anger at a future time.

Some people handle anger by *expressing* it. By use of the word "expression" I do not at this point mean discussion in a calm manner. I am referring to an outburst of anger, to pouting or to giving someone the silent treatment. When you express your anger you let others know you're angry.

A good many people today think that is the way to handle anger. If you express it you're letting people know how you really feel, "letting it all hang out." But it's interesting to note that psychologists are slowly backing off from recommending that behavior because they're recognizing that anger is like a snowball rolling down a hillside. The longer it continues, the bigger it gets. Similarly, expressing anger in an obvious manner, as if the anger is completely justified, simply makes the anger grow larger and the expression more vehement. We don't understand why, but expressing anger without any consideration for others does not lessen anger; it increases it. As a result, simply expressing your anger to those around you is not a good solution to anger, because it creates further problems.

Finally, a person can *confess* anger. The reason I suggest confession rather than expression is that confession contains an element of sorrow. Confession means that you face up to your anger by admitting to the people involved that you're angry and by telling them why you're angry. If the anger is not justified, you confess to make a clean breast of what it was that you responded to when you became angry. On the other hand, if your anger is justified, your confession says that you're sorry it's necessary to be angry, but you're going to use your anger to correct the problem you see. Your anger, then, is a warning that according to you something is wrong, and you want it corrected. You don't use your anger as a club, but simply show that you'll do whatever you can to correct this bad situation. Your anger will not disappear until the situation has been corrected.

Assignment: (1) Using the following chart, number from one to four the methods you use in dealing with anger (one is for the most frequent, and four is for the least frequent).

_____ Repress
_____ Suppress
_____ Express
_____ Confess

(2) Using another piece of paper, note all instances of anger this week. Analyze the context of your anger. What happened before you got angry? What were the events you reacted against when you became angry? What thoughts went through your mind about that event leading to your anger? Note also the method you used with your anger. Note whether it was effective or ineffective. Note also whether it was a wise choice. Give reasons for your answer. This will prepare you for the next chapter.

NINE
Dealing with Anger

How do you handle anger? Do you repress it and let it attack you through guerrilla warfare? Do you suppress it and handle it at a later time? Do you express it and let everyone around dive for cover when you get angry? Or do you confess it, seeking to deal honestly with the anger? This last approach is what I want to argue for in this chapter. The ability to deal with anger in ways that destroy neither you nor others is an important part of assertiveness. Fear of or inability to control anger prevents many people from being assertive. So now let's consider how to deal effectively with anger by confessing it.

ADMIT YOUR ANGER

The first step in effectively handling anger is admitting that you're angry. Simple though that may sound, it's really not easy. The Bible tells us, "The heart is deceitful above all things, and desperately corrupt; who can understand it?" (Jer. 17:9). Many people don't realize when they're angry. They don't even realize afterward that they *were* angry. All of us get angry sometime or other without realizing it. As a result, admitting you're angry isn't easy. You need help recognizing it—the help of others. Many times this help will be unknowing on their part. They won't realize they're helping you, even when they are. At other times you'll listen to what others tell you in order to learn that you're angry.

Let's look first at the unconscious help people give when you're angry. How can people unknowingly help you? There are a number of ways. First, is the person to whom you're talking getting angry? If so, that may be a sign that you're angry. Anger generates anger (Prov. 15:1). This means that if the person to whom you're talking is beginning to get angry, he might be responding to your anger. At that point you can either assume you're angry and back off, or you can ask a simple question: "Do I appear to be angry to you right now?" If the person says yes, you should trust his judgment.

This is particularly true if the listener is a member of your family. A basic principle of family communication is that other members of your family know your emotional states better than you do. If a member of your family tells you you're angry, he's probably right, even if you don't agree.

Other people tell you by their sudden silence. If you begin a discussion with someone and he suddenly becomes silent, you're probably angry. Many people won't talk with an angry person. They recognize they'll get nowhere, so they simply quit speaking. So if people around you quit talking after you've spoken, you're probably angry.

Closely related is withdrawal. If when you're talking with a person he suddenly gives very short answers to your statements, and you can almost physically see him withdraw, take it as a sign that you're angry. Most people don't like to fight, so when they see a fight coming—anger—they pull their heads into a shell, withdrawing just like a turtle.

You need more help, though, than people's unconscious reactions. There are people who can communicate directly that you're angry. I already mentioned members of your family. When they ask why you're angry, there's no use denying it; you're angry and had better face it. If you ask close friends to help you, they can give you a prearranged signal to let you know you're angry. If you give them a chance, they can be very helpful.

Prayer should also play a role in helping you discover your anger. The psalmist David recognized the deceitfulness of his own heart when he prayed, "Search me, O God, and know my heart! Try me and know my thoughts! And see if there be any hurtful [margin] way in me" (Psalm 139:23, 24). He knew that God alone could fully expose the hurtful ways in his life.

Similarly, as you face the destructive nature of your anger, prayer alone will reveal the many times anger influences your action. As God reveals your anger through your prayers, you can more effectively work at controlling it.

But there are a number of things you can do for yourself to help you discover when you're angry. We all have special behavior patterns we follow. For example, when I get angry, I immediately lower my voice and talk very softly with people. I carefully measure my words, sometimes almost choking because I am working so hard to control myself. My pulse begins to run as my heart beats faster and faster. I sometimes feel flushed and warm.

What do you do when you're angry? Some people speak louder. Some tense their muscles, particularly making fists or opening and closing their hands. Some people have difficulty breathing; some get very dry mouths and find it difficult to talk. In extreme instances, some people stutter or become tongue-tied and unable to speak; others develop tics.

To learn how to control your anger, you need to discover just what it is you do when you become angry. That will help you see your anger, which is the first step in the direction of admitting you're angry. Write down on a piece of paper those things you do when you get angry.

YOU ARE WHAT YOU THINK

The second step in dealing with anger is to ask yourself a question: "What am I doing to make myself angry?" Remember, we have assumed from the beginning of this book that no one else is responsible for your emotions. No one else can make you angry. You get angry because of what you tell yourself in response to an event in your life. Thus, this question focuses on the real problem. What are you telling yourself that is making you angry?

Think of one time last week when you were angry. Write out what you told yourself that made you angry. Now examine the statement in detail. Is it logical? Is it a real picture of what was happening? Would other people support your statement? Is there another interpretation that puts the event in a better light? Challenge the validity of your statement until you can produce half a dozen good ideas that will show that you are wrong to be angry. (Obviously, this applies to those situations in which anger is wrong and not justified.) I cannot emphasize enough the importance of challenging your statements that make you angry.

For example, let's imagine that a car cut in front of you as you drove past the shopping center. You felt an immediate surge of anger. Why? What were you telling yourself that made you angry? You may have said inwardly, *That sure was a stupid thing to do. I can't stand people who do stupid things.* Or you might have said to yourself, *He almost caused an accident. The kids might have been seriously hurt if I hadn't been able to swerve around him.* In the first instance, you convinced yourself that the appropriate response to stupid behavior is anger. Thus, whenever anyone does something you consider stupid, you're justified in becoming angry. In the second instance, you told yourself that this person almost injured your children. You believe that anger is an appropriate response when someone almost injures your children. In each instance, these ideas can be challenged.

Your response to stupid behavior could be a desire to help the person overcome the ignorance that led to his stupid behavior. It could also be that you want to do something that will eliminate stupid people from the highways. Anger is not the logical response to stupid behavior; there are many other things you could do.

Similarly, anger is not the only logical response to near injury for your children. There are many other things you could tell yourself that would prevent anger. You could immediately thank God that he kept you from harm. That's an equally logical response. You could use the incident as a teaching moment for your children, showing them what happens when a person acts without consideration for others.

What you tell yourself about what happens to you determines the way you will respond. That's why it's so important for you to analyze the statements you make to yourself that cause you to get angry.

Having determined what you said, you now have an obligation to challenge those statements. Only by showing yourself that your statements are wrong can you make statements that will change your emotional response from anger to something more appropriate.

SLOW DOWN

The third step in effectively handling anger is to develop ways to make yourself slow to anger (James 1:19, 20). We jokingly speak about counting to ten before getting angry, but it really isn't a bad idea. If you count to ten you have time to think. Think by using active listening to help delay anger. That way you keep yourself from getting angry when you really don't understand what the other person said.

Another good way to delay anger is to take five deep breaths. That both relaxes you and again gives you time to think.

Another excellent way is to figure out a question you can politely ask the other person that will help him expand on the subject getting you angry. By doing this you often get more insight into what is happening and have less justification for your anger.

What can you think of? What behavior can you plan that will make it more difficult for you to get angry quickly? Write out your battle plan for the next time you sense yourself becoming angry. Then put your plan into action.

COMMUNICATE YOUR ANGER

Fourth, everyone should learn to communicate his feelings of anger in a nonthreatening manner. Ephesians 4:25 says we should speak the truth in love. It's possible to communicate to another person, using I-messages, a low-threat message that you are angry. To do this is only to be honest. If you use an I-message, you also communicate that you have no plan to attack the other person but want help in overcoming your anger. You might say, "Can we pause for a minute? I feel angry about what I just heard you say [or what you did], and I need help dealing with that anger." This gives the other person a chance to help you—which we all like to do—while at the same time involving the one who is a party to your anger in its solution. By revealing your feelings, you don't have to get into a fight, as some people think. You can be honest and have it lead to a good discussion that will clear the air and eliminate your anger.

I recently had a conversation with the police about a potential child abuse case. When I gave them the information I had, the officer in charge said, "Oh, that's not our business. Take that to the Department of Social Services." I responded, "You know, my immediate response to your statement is anger. It appears to me that you are hiding from your responsibility." The officer then explained, "Not really. They have better investigative tools than we do for child abuse cases. If they discover through their investigation a law violation, then they turn the evidence over to us for our follow-up." As you can see, I expressed my anger in the least threatening way possible, and the officer responded by handling my anger without offense.

Remember, however, to be assertive, not aggressive, in expressing your anger. The reason anger is so frequently destructive is that people use it aggressively; they attack the other person. If you communicate assertively, however, letting the other person know exactly why you're angry, you can work toward a solution of your problem.

OVERCOME YOUR ANGER

Finally, work to overcome your anger. If you're talking to another person and having a disagreement about something, begin with a promise not to attack him. Tell him you want to solve the problem, not take him apart in the process. That assurance goes a long way toward making certain that your anger will be overcome, not enlarged.

After you've promised not to attack, seek to clarify the cause of your anger. What happened? What did you hear? What did you say to yourself? How does this relate to similar events in the past? What happened earlier in the day to prepare the way for this surge of emotion? Listen actively to what the other person is saying. All this is necessary to discover the real cause of your anger so you don't end up discussing a side issue.

If the other person is not actually present when you get angry, visualize an assertive response when you talk with him. Remember, be assertive, not aggressive. Figure out just what you plan to say so that you won't permit your emotions to overcome your desire to solve the problem with a mutually acceptable solution. Visualize an effective assertive response. If you plan to fail you will, but if you plan to succeed, there is a good chance you will succeed.

In all of this, remember, however, that the person you talk with might not appreciate your expression of anger. He might have an entirely different perspective on the situation and might care little or not at all about your response. There are such people, and you'll meet them. An assertive response that honestly faces the situation does not guarantee success, but it does provide the best possible method for working in that direction.

If the other person is only interested in getting his own way, you might end up in a win-lose conflict. At that point, you have to determine what you want and act accordingly. Sometimes you will withdraw; sometimes you will fight almost to the death. What I am concerned about is that you be able to choose those situations rather than be forced into them because you failed to communicate in an assertive, Christian manner.

What happens when you fail to deal with anger in a proper way? You either attack the other person, pout for days, or simply walk away and brood about what happened, carrying on your own guerrilla warfare against the person with whom you are angry.

In other words, your anger becomes sin.

Most books I've seen dealing with anger fail to address this subject. Even as I write on anger, I recognize that I sometimes become angry and don't handle situations well (probably more often than I care to admit). What do you do when you fail to handle anger in a Christian way? Repent! There is no other appropriate response.

How do you repent? Let's look at this in detail. Inability to repent effectively causes a lot of future angry responses, because you have not been forgiven for your past angry responses. The basic Scripture behind this is Matthew 5:22–26:

But I say to you that every one who is angry with his brother shall be liable to judgment; whoever insults his brother shall be liable to the council, and whoever says, "You fool!" shall be liable to the hell of fire. So if you are offering your gift at the altar, and there remember that your brother has something against you, leave your gift there before the altar and go; first be reconciled to your brother, and then come and offer your gift. Make friends quickly with your accuser, while you are going with him to court, lest your accuser hand you over to the judge, and the judge to the guard, and you be put in prison; truly, I say to you, you will never get out till you have paid the last penny.

Jesus makes it clear in the Sermon on the Mount that if your brother has something against you—your anger—you have the responsibility to go to him and straighten it out. Here are the steps to follow.

CONFESS SINFUL ANGER

First, confess your sin to God. That isn't always easy. Because you know that anger is sometimes justified, there is a tendency to expand your idea of justifiable anger to what you have recently done. To set the climate for repentance, I sometimes find it helpful to meditate for a while on the effect my anger had on my brother. What trouble did it cause him? What hurt did he experience? How would I feel had I been the recipient of my anger? As I meditate on these thoughts, I find it much easier to come to God and confess my sin.

Do you stop when you have confessed your sin to God? No, that would not be right. When you have injured another person, you have the responsibility to ask forgiveness from that person, just as you ask forgiveness from God. This is a greatly neglected Christian teaching. Even more neglected is the method for asking another person to forgive you. Let's examine that in detail.

Before you ask another person to forgive you, carefully think about what you're going to say. Sometimes you should even write out what you want to say to keep your emotions from getting in the way and further complicating the problem. Be very careful to include two key phrases when you ask for forgiveness. First, always say, "I was wrong." Follow that with a brief statement of what you did that was wrong. Never imply by anything you say that the other person caused you to behave as you did; that would be a lie.

The second key phrase is your conclusion, "Would you

forgive me?" And make certain you get an answer. Most people will respond the first time with, "Well, it wasn't really that big a deal." Or they'll say, "Sure, what's the difference? It didn't really matter." But those responses are not right. It did matter or you would not be confessing your sin. Sin is not something to be taken lightly. You need (more desperately than you usually realize) to hear the other person say, "Yes, I forgive you." At that point you are reconciled. Before that your need to confess has not been taken seriously, nor has the other person's need to forgive you. Reconciliation cannot occur until you hear those words, "I forgive you."

The first time you go to another to ask for forgiveness is particularly difficult. For that reason, I suggest that you write out your planned confession ahead of time. I would also offer some important warnings. Don't treat this matter through the mail if there is any way you can talk to the person face to face. Also, don't handle the matter over the phone if you can talk to the person face to face. This is too important for a telephone call.

Next, be brief. The other person doesn't need a long explanation of what happened. He was there and probably remembers the details of what happened far better than you do. (One time I asked a man's forgiveness and he said, "I forgot about that long ago." He then proceeded to give me details of the event that *I* had long since forgotten!)

Finally, be humble. Nothing ruins a confession quicker than a superior attitude. If you think that by your confession you're in any way better than the other person, you will subvert the whole process. Be humble as you confess your wrong and ask forgiveness.

Assignment: (1) Write out the signs of anger in your life if you have not already done so. Be specific. Then learn to recognize them when they appear and to handle the anger that comes at those times.

(2) Clear the past of all wrongs resulting from prior instances of anger. Until you do that, a change from an angry person to a calm person will never be accepted by those around you. They'll think, as they often do about an alcoholic who has reformed, *It's just a matter of time until he reverts*

back to his old ways. Confession of your anger from the past will provide a barricade against anger in the future. Lay out a plan for seeking reconciliation with all those people who are estranged from you because of your anger. That may take a long time, but it's well worth the effort.

TEN
Dealing with Anxiety

Why aren't you as assertive as you would like to be? Why do you sometimes let others manipulate you? Why do you sometimes react in anger to a situation in which hindsight tells you there was no reason for anger? The answer is anxiety.

When you feel anxious, you often do things you really don't want to do. Remember how we saw in the first chapter that people often manipulate you by making you feel guilty, ignorant, or anxious? I can't do much to help you feel guilt-free or knowledgeable in every situation you face. I can only suggest that you learn how to counter those thoughts with a realistic evaluation of the situation. Anxiety is frequently not a feeling that arises at the moment of confrontation, but a feeling that's around for a long time before you speak to another. Therefore, we can deal specifically with anxiety in a much more extensive way.

Worry and anxiety are the two biggest reasons people don't act assertively. Most people would rather avoid the feeling of anxiety than face it and solve the problem confronting them. This may be shortsighted; it may only solve the immediate problem and leave the long-term problem unsolved, but most people would rather relieve their immediate anxiety than face the problem directly and solve the long-term problem.

Let's assume, for example, that you know you're not being

paid enough for the work you're doing. You've compared your salary to the salaries of others working around you doing the same thing, and you've discovered that they're earning more. That upsets you greatly, but you're afraid to face your boss. The very thought makes your insides churn; you imagine all the things that might go wrong. He might get upset and fire you; he might become angry and demote you; he might refuse to give you your vacation next month. All sorts of things go through your mind, causing you to feel anxious about the confrontation.

As a result, to avoid the immediate anxiety you would experience in talking with your boss, you decide not to say anything. That means, however, that you'll live with a continuing feeling that you're being taken advantage of. The short-term problem—anxiety—you solve; but the long-term problem—your mistreatment—remains. Unless you're willing to face your anxiety and work in spite of it, you'll never solve the long-term problem.

WORRY AND ANXIETY

Before we go further, what's the difference between worry and anxiety? Although up until now I've used the words synonymously, I'd like to change and make a distinction between them. When I speak about worry I am talking about concern over a real problem. In reality, your feeling about going and talking to the boss about a raise is worry because it has a specific focus. The boss might actually fire you if you confront him about the difference between your salary and the salaries of your co-workers. He might not give you your vacation next month. The focus of your worry is a very real situation.

Anxiety, on the other hand, is a generalized feeling of tension or sense that something is wrong—almost a feeling of dread. Anxiety produces many of the same physical symptoms as worry. You are preoccupied with your problem; you find it difficult to concentrate on other things; you might have an upset stomach, headaches, allergy flare-ups, nervous tics, stuttering, or all sorts of other problems indicative of worry. Nonetheless, there is a major difference. When you worry you can write down on a sheet of paper the things you are worrying about. When you're anxious, you can't. If someone asks what's wrong, you don't really have an answer. There's nothing concrete that you can point to and say, "This is the problem."

In real life, however, worry and anxiety cannot always be so neatly separated. They often mingle. When you go to talk to the boss about a raise, you might worry about all the things mentioned earlier. But let's suppose the boss is an easygoing fellow who never gets angry with anyone. Every time in the past that you asked him for a raise, he gave it to you. The one exception was when the business was having problems, but even then he thoroughly explained the situation before finally saying no. He has never refused you a day off when you've asked for it. Now, does that mean that when you go to ask for a raise you will be calm, cool, and collected? No, it doesn't! Any time you talk to somebody about something important, particularly when you feel injured by the other person's behavior, you experience anxiety. Anxiety is bad, then, only when it is excessive, when it prevents you from doing what you want to do.

As a minister, I do a good deal of public speaking. I can honestly say that I've never entered the pulpit, no matter how thoroughly I prepared, without experiencing anxiety. Having spoken with other ministers, some of them highly successful, I've learned that no good speaker enters the pulpit without feeling anxious.

But I've also learned something else. There are some ministers who confess that they feel perfectly calm and relaxed when they enter the pulpit. According to their testimony, they have absolutely no feelings of anxiety. I can also say that I've rarely heard anything worthwhile from these men. Their lack of anxiety indicates a lack of concern about what they're doing.

All this leads me to conclude that a certain measure of anxiety is good for us. If we experience no anxiety, then in certain situations we lack the drive to succeed, to do a good job. We are concerned not about anxiety by itself, then, but about anxiety that keeps us from doing what we really want to do. That kind of anxiety needs to be overcome.

DEALING WITH WORRY

Let's get back now to the problem of worry. How do you handle worry? Is there something specific you can do as a means of overcoming worry? Yes. The pattern is very similar to what I suggested earlier.

Worry has a focus. Therefore, the first thing you should do when you discover that you're worrying about something is to write down all the reasons why you're worrying. Don't be concerned at this time about whether they're good or bad reasons for worrying. They're your reasons, and right now that's what is important. Write down every possible thought you have that's making you worry.

Now take your worries one by one and examine their truthfulness. Write down the worry at the top of a sheet of paper, and under the worry write five or six reasons why there's no reason for worrying about that problem. Do this with each of the worries you have.

Before we go to the third step, let's examine something that might happen in step two. Let's assume that you discover that one of your worries is very real. You are worrying about what would happen if you asked your boss for a raise. You know that the last man in your plant who did that was asked to find another job. As a result, you are worrying about whether you would also be asked to leave if you asked for a raise. As you examine this problem, you might see that the man was not doing his job and the boss used his request for a raise as an excuse to fire him. But it might be that the boss just doesn't like people to ask for a raise, no matter what the reason.

How do you handle your worry when the worry is real? First, you examine the consequences of your proposed plan of action. Is the possibility of being fired worth the raise? Are there better jobs in other plants just for asking? Is there a chance the boss will propose a raise for you without your requesting it? Such questions help you eliminate the worry by facing the problem directly.

Second, however, you lay out a plan of action. Either you decide it isn't worth the bother to ask for the raise and you forget about it, seek another job, or whatever, or you make a plan to speak with your boss. You select the right time of day, the right day of the week, and you plan what you're going to say and how you will respond to his expected questions. Having done that, you follow out your plan of action. That eliminates the worry. You simply go and do what has to be done, although you will still experience anxiety.

For the Christian, the third step in facing worry involves prayer. Many verses speak to us at this point, but particularly Philippians 4:6, 7: "Don't worry about anything, but in all things by prayer and entreaty with gratitude let your requests be known to God. And God's peace, beyond all understanding, will sustain your hearts and minds in Christ Jesus" (author's paraphrase). What can be clearer than that your worry is overcome by talking with God about it to gain his perspective? You need to take your worries to God in prayer.

The fourth step in overcoming worry is to create another STOP! card. Whenever you find yourself worrying about the problem, get out the STOP! card. If you're by yourself, actually say out loud, "STOP!" In this way you break out of the pattern of worrying.

But remember, you can't just push negative thoughts from your mind, and you can't just push worry out of your mind, either. You have to replace your worrisome thoughts with wholesome thoughts. That's the fifth step.

Plan a positive counterthought for when you catch yourself worrying. As a Christian, you should turn immediately to a Bible verse that talks about worry. Jesus' statement about God's caring for our every need in Matthew 6:25-33 is excellent. Many people find effective this simple verse: "Cast all your anxieties on him for he cares about you" (1 Pet. 5:7). That verse shows why you shouldn't worry. You should be giving your cares to God so that he who made the world can bear them for you.

But you should do more than simply quote a Bible verse. Although meditating on the Bible verse should certainly be your first move, examining and thinking about your counterthoughts is also effective. Think about the statements of worry you made. Now think about all the different ideas you proposed to counter your worry, and meditate on those. As you do that, the Bible verse and your counterthoughts will slowly force your worries out of your mind until they no longer dominate you.

You also need to remember what progress means. Remember that you are progressing in your worry-stopping activity when you worry less frequently, for shorter periods of time, or with less intensity. So keep a record. Note how often you worry and with what intensity. Then note the changes that take place in your worry pattern. Any one or all of these areas should diminish during the coming week as you put this plan into action.

DEALING WITH ANXIETY

Now we approach the difficult task—how to overcome anxiety. First, remember that anxiety is not always bad; there are times when it's necessary. This leads to our first step: What level of anxiety should you experience in a particular situation? If you are about to speak or play a musical instrument for the first time in front of an audience, a high level of anxiety is to be anticipated. But if you are lying on the beach on a nice summer day, absorbing the sun and the beauty of the day, and you're highly anxious, something is wrong. Again, what level of anxiety do you think you should be experiencing in your particular situation?

Psychologists have recently developed a scale that's helpful in determining your expected level of anxiety. It's called the SUDS scale (Subjective Unit of Disturbance Scale). You use the SUDS scale to help you determine what your expected level of anxiety is. To begin, imagine a scale of from 0 to 100. Zero represents how you feel when you're completely relaxed. Imagine in your own mind the most relaxing situation you can picture. Mentally put yourself in that situation. Imagine how you feel at that time. That's how you feel when you score 0. Now imagine a situation in which you would be highly anxious, more anxious than in any other situation you can imagine. Mentally place yourself in that situation. That's your 100 score. All other experiences fall between 0 and 100.

For example, imagine that you are going to ask your boss for an extra day off next week. Where should you place your expected level of anxiety—30? 50? 90? Or let's say you want to ask your brother to loan you $1000 to get you out of some financial difficulties. Where would you expect your anxiety level to fall? 50? 80? 95? Every event that causes you anxiety can be ranked, but only you can do it. In addition, only you can tell how low you want your SUDS score to be at any given time. It is a highly subjective, yet valuable, tool to help you determine what would satisfy you.

Now let's examine four other criteria that help determine your anxiety level. They are eye contact, posture, nervous laughter or joking, and excessive or unrelated head, hand, and body movements.

First consider *eye contact.* Your anxiety level can readily be determined by your eye contact, because when you're relaxed you look at another person's eyes as you talk. When you begin to look away at the floor, the ceiling, or things around the room, your avoidance of eye contact indicates anxiety.

The second criterion is *posture.* This measure has extremes, however, rather than a continuum. Your posture should be appropriate for the particular conversation or situation you're in. You cannot be speaking in public and be perfectly relaxed. On the other hand, you can't be so tense that you're unable to speak. The appropriateness or inappropriateness of your posture indicates your anxiety level.

A third criterion is *nervous laughter or joking.* When these appear, they indicate anxiety. We've all seen this. A friend is in a very serious situation—for example, talking to a policeman about a traffic violation—and the person giggles and makes silly jokes. You can't believe your eyes or ears, but that's what you see. When a person laughs where it isn't appropriate, or jokes when jokes are out of order, it usually indicates anxiety.

The final criterion is *excessive or unrelated head, hand, and body movements.* Again, public speaking brings this out effectively. We've all seen a public speaker who talks while constantly playing with something in his pocket. Or we've seen a speaker who uses excessive gestures, wholly inappropriate to what he says. I once witnessed a minister in this situation who looked like a windmill when he talked. Finally, I had to stare at the floor and listen only to the content of his message, which was excellent. His gestures, however, indicated that he was highly anxious about his ability to perform.

When you combine these four physical criteria with your SUDS score, you have a fair measure of your anxiety. You can then ask yourself the question, "Am I excessively anxious at this time, or is my anxiety level appropriate?" You alone can determine this for yourself. Is an anxiety level of 70 appropriate when I ask my boss for a raise? Would 35 be more appropriate? Only you can determine whether your anxiety is too high and is hindering your effectiveness. But once you've determined whether it's appropriate, you can then determine what you want to do about it.

Even though I earlier said that anxiety is causeless, the second step, after you have determined your anxiety level, is still to find a cause for your anxiety. Are you simply anxious rather than worried? If you are worried, if there is a cause for your feelings, you should return to the steps for handling worry. Again, if your anxiety is what anyone would expect in the same situation, there is nothing to be done. But if your anxiety is too high or totally causeless, you have reason to act.

The plan is quite simple, for it's exactly what I prescribed to handle worry. Create another STOP! card. Whenever you sense you're becoming anxious, bring out the card. Use a Bible verse on the back such as Philippians 4:6, 7: "Have no anxiety about anything, but in everything by prayer and supplication with thanksgiving let your requests be made known to God. And the peace of God, which passes all understanding, will keep your hearts and your minds in Christ Jesus." In addition, develop counterthoughts to combat your anxiety.

In dealing with anxiety, because it's often causeless, you might need help. Dealing with anxiety is not something most people can do on their own. Therefore, if anxiety is a long-term problem with you, I suggest that you talk with your pastor about it or see some other professional counselor. The help he would be able to give would take a big step toward overcoming your difficulty. Anxiety is debilitating. Overcoming it is a significant part of becoming assertive, of coming to the point that you can choose how you will act rather than permitting others to manipulate you.

LEARN TO RELAX

Many people have trouble with anxiety because they've never learned how to relax. Psychologists have developed a method to help people learn how to relax, first in private, then in public as you sense anxiety levels rising. This exercise is called deep muscle relaxation. First, tense the muscles in each group listed below in the order given. Tense the muscles for five to seven seconds. At the end of that time, let the muscle completely relax for twenty to thirty seconds. Do this for each of the muscle groups listed.

Use this method for twenty to thirty minutes each day. Find a place where you can be by yourself, preferably in a reclining position. It's best if you can put the exercise on recording tape, leaving blank tape following each instruction to give yourself time to tense and relax.

Below is the order of major muscle groups to be relaxed (taken from Merna D. Galassi and John P. Galassi, *Assert Yourself,* Human Science Press, 1977, pp. 70, 71):

1. Tense the muscles in your right hand by making a fist.
2. Tense the muscles in your right upper arm. Bend your arm at the elbow and make a muscle.
3. Tense the muscles in your left hand by making a fist.
4. Tense the muscles in your left upper arm. Bend your arm at the elbow and make a muscle.
5. Tense the muscles in your forehead by frowning.
6. Tense the muscles in your eyes by closing your eyes tightly.
7. Tense the muscles in your nose by wrinkling it.
8. Tense the muscles in your lips and lower face by pressing your lips together tightly and forcing your tongue against the top of your mouth.
9. Tense the muscles in your jaw by clenching your teeth together.
10. Tense the muscles in your neck by attempting to look directly above you.
11. Tense the muscles in your shoulders and upper back by shrugging your shoulders.
12. Tense the muscles in your chest by taking a deep breath and holding it.
13. Tense the muscles in the small of your back by arching up your back.

14. Tense the muscles in your abdomen by either pushing those muscles out or pulling them in.
15. Tense the muscles in your buttocks and thighs by pressing your heels into the floor.
16. Tense the muscles in your ankles and calves by pointing them away from your body.

After a while, you'll find yourself relaxing without any difficulty. Then you can transfer the exercise to everyday life. When you sense tenseness in a particular muscle group, you'll be able to focus your mind on that group and consciously relax it. This does wonders in reducing tension and, with it, anxiety. I have used this method for years in the pulpit and found it quite helpful.

Assignment: (1) Work this week on overcoming a specific worry. (2) Practice the relaxation exercise once each day.

ELEVEN
Do You Like Yourself?

Do you like yourself? That certainly is a strange question, isn't it? Are there really people who don't like themselves? I'm afraid there are. In fact, I'd go so far as to say there are probably more people who dislike themselves than people who do like themselves. In fact, recent studies have shown that more than half the adult women in the country admit that one of their biggest problems is their self-image. They don't feel good about what they are or what they're doing.

How does self-image relate to the problem of asserting yourself? Can a poor self-image keep you from asserting yourself? It certainly can.

A person with a poor self-image feels unsure of himself. Because he has rejected himself, he often thinks others will reject him. As a result, he will either behave passively, letting others take advantage of him, or he will behave aggressively to hide his lack of self-confidence. Either way, his poor self-image prevents him from expressing his feelings, desires, or opinions in a nonthreatening way. Thus, a major pillar of assertive behavior is a good feeling about yourself.

Although the number of people with poor self-images might surprise you, it's really not surprising. Our society has programmed most of us for failure since the day we were born. It did this completely unconsciously, but nonetheless, it did it. How?

SOCIETY'S STANDARDS

Society has established three rather rigid standards to determine whether you are a worthwhile person. If you do not measure up in one of these ways, you'll be judged less than a success, possibly even a failure. These three standards are *appearance, achievement,* and *status.* Unless you excel in one of these areas, you're not a success. Because most of us have lived in no other society than the one we now live in, we've accepted these standards, entirely unconsciously, as our standards. We judge other people by them just as harshly as they judge us. But we also judge ourselves, and we sometimes do that far more harshly than others would ever think of doing. The epitome of the first standard, appearance, is found in the annual Miss America Pageant. Here we look for the nicest-appearing girl in the United States. We might include a lot of other criteria for determining who will be the next Miss America, but when all is said and done, they don't choose ugly but highly talented young women. This is a contest to determine who is most beautiful.

We find this same value judgment in many of the toys our children purchase, from Barbie doll to Superman. Each of these dolls is exquisitely formed (according to our cultural standards). *Playboy* is another wonderful example as they use airbrushes to remove any possible blemishes from their centerfolds. They want nothing to mar the appearance of their beauties.

The problem with contests like beauty pageants and a standard that judges on appearance is that only the exceptional can be judged successful. By definition, the vast majority of the population cannot measure up. The average person is average; therefore, according to the standard, he is not worthwhile or valuable. Only those having outstanding appearance will measure up.

Although this standard may be personally devastating, it is economically profit-producing. It means that the vast majority of the people will spend time and money to make themselves as much like the most beautiful people as possible. They will buy clothes, cosmetics, hairstyles, and hundreds of other items in an attempt to measure up to the standard that only a few can meet. Nonetheless, the vast majority of the population fails to measure up. As a result, those people feel inferior; often they do not like themselves.

The second standard established by our society is achievement. The prime example of this is *People* magazine. This magazine brings together under one cover the achievers of this world. We experience their success vicariously by reading about what they have done. We Christians do the same when we gobble up books about successful fellow believers. All this says that we have entered into the fray just as much as the world. We also judge people by their achievements.

But as with appearance, there is a major problem. Only a select few will achieve at a high enough level to stand out above all others. The average person remains average. Most of us will not achieve sufficiently to gain recognition. We will judge ourselves failures, even as we judge others failures who do not achieve.

As noted before, we are frequently harsher, far more judgmental in viewing ourselves, than others. It has been my experience as I have had occasion to meet "successful" Christians that most of them suffer in this way. Although everyone else in the Christian world may view them as successful, they constantly struggle with their own feelings of failure because they judge themselves so harshly.

The final standard is status. It's frequently true that the person who is beautiful will have status, and it's true that most people who stand out for their achievements will also enjoy status. But status can also come through position. A minister has status no matter how successful or beautiful; a town mayor has status, even though unsuccessful and not beautiful. This is true even if the town has only 350 people; status comes with being mayor. There are many other similar positions. Wealth also confers status. There is more room for recognition by society at this point than at any other.

But again, the vast majority of people will not have any status. Even in that little community of 350, there is only one mayor and probably only two or three ministers. Most people lack status, which brings us again to the fact that the average person is average. Such being the case, most people do not receive recognition from others, and therefore they feel like failures, or at least unsuccessful. This often means they don't like themselves or have problems with what we call a poor self-image.

Complicating all this is the normal response to people who are beautiful, have achieved something notable, or have status. When you look at another person and compare yourself to him, you look at one of his strongest points and usually contrast that with one of your weakest points. As a minister, I could conceivably be the best preacher in my state. But if another man comes and gives a beautiful number in song that moves the congregation to tears, I will feel insignificant because I can't do the same. I consider myself a failure because he can sing better than I, even though I may be able to preach better than the thousands of other ministers in the state. By comparing your weak points with others' strengths, you guarantee your failure before you begin. Your weak points will never come out favorably when compared with another's strengths.

YOUR FEELINGS OF INFERIORITY

I recently took a seminary class with a few other ministers. During the class I met a minister about my own age who pastors a church in Texas with weekly attendance approaching 1,200. I pastor a church with a weekly attendance of less than 100. As we talked, I told him that I felt inferior and less than successful in his presence because he pastored a church much larger than my own. He laughed and replied, "I feel inferior to you because you've published a book and I haven't." Each of us compared himself with the other in an area in which he felt weak. We both have strengths that we could enjoy, but when we got together we simply had to put ourselves down by comparing the other's "success" in one area to our "failure" in another. How foolish!

Few people realize how strongly they are attached to these standards. I can point out that they are totally unbiblical, and I can add that they are irrational because they guarantee failure for most people—but we still use them. Why?

The reasons are probably found in the nature of human development. As you grow up you live in a world of giants, supersophisticated giants, even though you don't realize it at the time. Your parents were far bigger than you and therefore far stronger. They were much smarter because of their years of experience; therefore, any time you got into an argument, you had to lose. And they were much more skillful than you, which means that they were always showing you up in most anything you attempted to do. Growing up under those conditions laid a solid foundation for your feelings that everyone else can do, be, or look better than you.

Similarly, many parents while rearing their children do things to them that create feelings of inadequacy. They berate their children for their lack of skills or knowledge; they never compliment their children for their successes; and they frequently make critical comments about them. All these things create a feeling of failure, of the inability to measure up. This feeling, developed early in childhood, often remains with a person for the rest of his life unless something conscious is done to fight it.

Here is an exercise to help you see the effect of your childhood. Think back to your childhood and remember an event that you see had both a negative effect at the time and a negative influence that remains to the present day. Write that event out. When you are finished writing it out and thinking of its present effect, write five or six statements that challenge the effect of the event. If you can do that with a number of different events, it may help overcome some of the negative influences of those events.

One of the results of the influence of your parental home is that you develop a way of seeing the world. If your parents frequently criticize you for being clumsy, you soon overlook all the times when you aren't clumsy and remember only those times when you are. You develop a file in your memory marked "Clumsy." Each time something important comes up that involves skill, you open the file, look at the record, and decide to avoid the event. Even now you cannot overcome the idea that you're clumsy. You filter out all contrary evidence that might show you aren't clumsy.

You have many filters like this in your mind. Each of them carefully screens materials contradictory to your present pattern of thinking. As a result, even if overwhelming evidence were presented to show that you aren't what you think, you would filter it out. That is why changing your self-image is a slow process.

Your perceptual pattern works something like this: You were treated by your parents in certain ways; they drew attention to your various strong or weak points. You now hear only what is consistent with the past. You filter out all material that is not consistent with what you already know. You build the present on the past. If you have been told you're clumsy, you won't do anything that might contradict that thought.

If people continue to comment about how clumsy you are, you will continue to be clumsy. (Thankfully, if someone close, such as your spouse, slowly guides you through a series of experiences in which you demonstrate skill, you can learn to change your thinking.) And as people see the way you act, you reinforce the way they think about you. As a result, your self-image is a circle. You begin by being what you were told you are, others see what you are, you hear what they say, and you behave in a manner consistent with what they say. The circle goes on and on until you make a conscious effort, often with someone else's help, to break the pattern.

Only active effort on your part will break the pattern. You cannot sit back and say, "Someday things will change when I succeed at something important." It just doesn't happen that way. You'll succeed at something important when you decide it's important enough to put forth the necessary effort. Until then, you'll remain in the same circle created in your mind as a child. Only conscious effort on your part will overcome that.

WHO ARE YOU?

Let's pause for a moment to see where you are as a person. Rate yourself on a scale of one to ten. One stands for a horrible or worthless person, and ten stands for someone fantastic. Be honest since no one else should see your answer unless you decide to reveal it.

Now, because most people base their self-image largely on the perceptions of others, I want you to do another exercise. List three people who know you well and love you anyhow. This should show you that even for you, success is not entirely determined by these false standards established by our world. People love us even when we don't succeed.

Now let's see what we can do to move in the direction of a positive self-image. To help you further in understanding where you are, do one more exercise. Complete this sentence ten times:

1. "I am . . . .
2. "I am . . . .
3. "I am . . . .
4. "I am . . . .
5. "I am . . . .
6. "I am . . . .
7. "I am . . . .
8. "I am . . . .
9. "I am . . . .
10. "I am . . . .

Are your comments positive or negative? Was this an easy exercise to do? Most people find it very difficult to finish the first time. We are uncomfortable talking about ourselves that way. That's too bad—it's also unbiblical. The Bible says very plainly that each of us should have a sane estimate of his capabilities (Rom. 12:3). That means that you should think of yourself neither more highly nor more lowly than you ought. Most of us fail in the second area. We think more lowly of ourselves than we ought. Try again. Can't you finish that sentence a few more times? There is nothing wrong with saying, "I am good . . . ," if it's true.

GOD VALUES YOU

But far more important than the way you complete those sentences is what the Bible has to say about you. First, you need to recognize that God created you and God doesn't make mistakes. That truth is given in many places in the Bible, but let's look at Psalm 139:13–16:

For thou didst form my inward parts, thou didst knit me together in my mother's womb. I praise thee, for thou are fearful and wonderful. Wonderful are thy works! Thou knowest me right well; my frame was not hidden from thee, when I was being made in secret, intricately wrought in the

*depths of the earth. Thy eyes beheld my unformed sub-
stance; in thy book were written, every one of them, the
days that were formed for me, when as yet there was none
of them.*

There are many paintings in this world, varying greatly in
their worth. In terms of the materials that went into them,
there is probably little variation in cost, but they vary greatly
in value because of the painter who painted them. That makes
the difference.

The same applies to you. You were created by the infinite
God who created this universe and everything in it. He is
perfect in all he does and says. You were created by him, and
that makes you infinitely valuable. In fact, apart from God
himself, there is nothing more valuable or important than
you. Other people may be equally important, but there is
nothing more important. That means that nothing you ever
achieve in your life will make you more valuable than you are
at present. Our society says, "Achieve status and we will
proclaim your life worth something." God says, "You are
valuable because I created you." What a wonderful assurance!

In 1 Peter 1:18, 19 we read, "You know that you were
ransomed from the futile ways inherited from your fathers,
not with perishable things such as silver or gold, but with the
precious blood of Christ, like that of a lamb without blemish
or spot." That shows your worth in another area. Our society
says, "Achieve status and we will proclaim your life worth
something." God says, "You have status because my Son died
for your sins." At this point we need to be careful that we do
not reverse this idea; Jesus did not die for us because of our
value. Even though we are God's creation, we are also sinners
worthy of his condemnation. But when Jesus died for us, by
his death he placed a great value upon us. That is the status
we now have.

Finally, Romans 8:14–17:

*For all who are led by the Spirit of God are sons of God. For
you did not receive the spirit of slavery to fall back into fear,
but you have received the spirit of sonship. When we cry,
"Abba! Father!" it is the Spirit himself bearing witness with
our spirit that we are children of God, . . . and fellow heirs*

with Christ, provided we suffer with him in order that we may also be glorified with him.

This passage says that we are members of God's family because we are Christians. Therefore, we belong. Again, the world says, "If you are a beautiful person we will welcome you." But God says, "As you have accepted Christ as your personal Savior, you are now a member of my family. You belong no matter what you do from this day forward. I accept you for who you are." Thus, we again see the great divergence from the world's standards. And after God accepts you, he then works with you at making you beautiful by helping you conform to the image of his Son. That's true beauty!

Is it wrong for a Christian to love himself, to think of himself as valuable? To answer that question, let's assume for a moment that the answer is no. First, the person who does not like himself usually lacks the confidence to do a job well, no matter what the job might be. He will quit too soon or strive for perfection, but in either instance, the job will not be done as it should be.

Second, the person who does not like himself will have difficulty standing up for what he thinks is right. He will allow wrong to prevail over right.

Finally, the Christian who does not like himself is judging God as inadequate. That's right. When a person says he is not good or worthwhile, he says God is wrong. How is that so? As God's creation, when you say you are not worthwhile, you are saying that God didn't know what he was doing when he created you. If only he would have anticipated your advice, or done things your way, everything would be all right. Few people have the audacity to say that, but it is implied in any criticism you make of the way you are constructed, whether with regard to looks, abilities, or even the place where you were brought up. To love yourself properly is to agree with God's evaluation of your life.

YOU ARE STILL WHAT YOU THINK

How does all this relate to changing your image of yourself? It all goes back to what I said about changing your thoughts.

You are what you think you are. If you think assertively, you will be assertive. If you think good thoughts about yourself, you will develop a good self-image. Secular psychologists at this point say you can improve your self-image by thinking over and over again, "I am valuable because I am me, and there is no one else like me." But that is like the boy who walks through the cemetery, talking with an imaginary friend to keep the ghosts from bothering him. It's nonsense, and anyone who thinks for a moment will realize it.

But the Bible gives the Christian a foundation for thinking good thoughts about himself. "I am valuable because God created me; I do not have to base my worth on what I can accomplish. I am valuable because God gave me value by sending his Son to die for my sins; I no longer have to search for stature. I have status as an object of God's love. I am further valuable because I'm a member of God's family. There is no more important "organization" in the world, and I am part of it. This means that I no longer have to look for acceptance based on my appearance. As I meditate on these things—good thoughts—I will slowly develop a good image of who I am. And that image will not be based on false standards, but on the reality of God's Word."

In Philippians 4:8, Paul says, "Finally, brethren, whatever is true, whatever is honorable, whatever is just, whatever is pure, whatever is lovely, whatever is gracious, if there is any excellence, if there is anything worthy of praise, think about these things." We see here that you are not to think about what you cannot do, but you're to praise God for, among many other things, the talents, abilities, and looks he has given you. As you concentrate on God, his love, and the blessings he's given you, he slowly transforms your life, giving you a beautiful spirit, the spirit of his Son. But that only happens when you concentrate your thinking on what is good, honorable, and excellent.

This all means that you need to change your thinking about yourself. You need to begin thinking positive, biblical thoughts about yourself.

We need to recognize the wisdom in the titles of two popular books, *The Power of Positive Thinking* and *Possibility Thinking*. If you think God's thoughts, you will become better. Again, this is no secular psychology baptized by a Christian writer for Christian readers. Paul tells us plainly in Philippians 4:8 that you should think good thoughts. And passages in the Old Testament promise success to those who meditate on *and obey* God's Word (Josh. 1:8; Psalm 1:1–3). You are what you think.

Assignment: (1) Memorize the passages that speak most to you about your self-image (Psalm 139:13–16; Rom. 8:14–17; 1 Pet. 1:18, 19). (2) Study the other passages, and make their thoughts part of your life.

TWELVE
How to Be Assertive

Have you found yourself becoming more assertive as you work through the material in this book? It may be that you haven't. Assertive behavior involves many different things. It involves attitudes on your part that let you feel comfortable with the idea of assertiveness. If you think it's wrong to assert yourself, you'll never be an assertive person. However, many people fail to be assertive because they've never learned how to handle their anger, because they're too anxious, or because they have such a poor image of themselves. As a result, I've spent more time dealing with these other problems than with telling you directly how to become more assertive. I've intentionally left specific assertive training until this next-to-the-last chapter because people cannot be assertive without having solved many of the problems we examined earlier. Now, if you've worked through the rest of the book, you're ready to begin.

RECOGNIZE YOUR WEAKNESS

First, memorize the assertive bill of rights. Unless you know when someone is violating your rights or someone else's, you won't be able to recognize your own nonassertive behavior. The first step toward assertiveness is learning to recognize violations of interpersonal rights and your own nonassertive behavior in the face of those violations. You also need to recognize other situations in which assertiveness is appropriate but in which you have failed in the past to be assertive (e.g., a potential witnessing situation).

How do you recognize nonassertive behavior? First, become aware of your feelings that lead to nonassertiveness. We saw earlier that people manipulate you by making you feel guilty, anxious, or ignorant. If they can do none of these things, they won't be able to manipulate you. Therefore, you need to learn to recognize your feelings as another person interacts with you. When you sense that you are feeling guilty, you have to discover for yourself if your anxiety is appropriate to the situation or if it is excessive. Only as you see this can you plan an assertive course of action.

Finally, you have to recognize when someone is making you feel ignorant. You have to be able, mentally, to stop the conversation and look at what is happening. Then, when you have determined why you are beginning to feel ignorant, you can begin to move in a direction that is assertive. You prevent others from manipulating you by challenging your feelings of guilt, anxiety, or ignorance, but you can't succeed until you learn to recognize those feelings.

In all this you have to listen to your own conversation. What are you saying that gives hints that you might be beginning to act nonassertively? ("I know I'm bothering you, but. . . .") What keys in your behavior point to nonassertive behavior? Do you lower your voice? Make excuses for what you want to do or say? Get highly nervous or tense? Avoid eye contact with other people? Begin to feel angry? Make apologies when you begin to explain what you believe in? What keys in your conversation tell you that you're beginning to behave nonassertively? Write them down for future reference.

Finally, be aware of your more common areas of failure. Assertive behavior is both situation-specific and person-specific. I hope that while reading this book you have begun to recognize that you are more assertive in some situations than in others. With friends you make requests that you would never make from your boss at work. With your family you say things that you would never say to your neighbors. You make demands on people at work that you don't make on members of your church. The person you are dealing with makes a great deal of difference in how assertive you are. You can be assertive with one person and fail to be assertive in an identical situation with another person. At the end of the chapter is a chart that will help you determine the categories of people with whom you have trouble being assertive.

Assertiveness is also determined by the situation. Most people find it easier to give a compliment than to receive one. It's usually easier to make a request from someone than to express a personal opinion. It's easier to express your opinion than to refuse a request. The most difficult situation for most people to be assertive in is when they need to express disagreement or feelings of displeasure or anger. Again, the chart at the end of the chapter will help you see the situations that cause you difficulty.

By being aware of the people and situations that cause you problems, you can prepare ahead of time for your nonassertive behavior; you can be more watchful. This means that you should plan ahead for those times when, or people with whom, you tend to behave nonassertively. If you have something important to discuss or work out, you need to put special thought into what you are going to say.

PLANNED BOLDNESS

First, think out what you want to say. Write it out in detail. If possible, write out what you think the other person would say in response. Further, do the same thing a number of different times until you think you have all the possible responses the other person would make. It's important to think out all possible responses so that you aren't surprised, no matter what comes up.

Even better than writing out your conversation is roleplaying with a friend. Have someone take the part of the person you will be talking to. Then carry on a conversation, letting the person respond in ways he thinks would be appropriate. To help you even more, take for yourself the part of the person you will talk to, and let your friend play your part. The more you practice, the more likely it is that you will manage to be assertive.

But set a deadline for your writing or practice. Because of anxiety—the natural desire to avoid a conflict—some people will practice and write until the second coming without acting. Set a time when you're going to talk to the person, and stick to it. Give yourself plenty of time to practice. (Two weeks seems like more than enough time.) But then go and talk.

I also suggest that you start practicing assertive behavior on less threatening people or in less threatening situations. For example, you might choose to give your spouse or children a compliment. That is certainly a low-threat situation with low-threat people. You might follow this up by making a request from someone around you who provides a low threat. You only slowly move up the scale to the point that you express a difference of opinion with your boss. Then, finally, you come to the most difficult point of expressing anger at people when it's called for.

You begin with simple situations because you want success (meaning you act assertively and others respond positively). You can only build a pattern of success if you begin where your success is almost assured and then move to those points where the possibility of success is more limited. If you begin small and experience success, you will eventually be able to handle the most difficult situations. It simply takes time and effort.

Assertiveness, as I suggested, is not something constant. You are not either an assertive or a nonassertive person; rather, you're assertive in some places and not in others. No matter how generally assertive a person might be, there will be areas in which the person will be nonassertive. For this reason I have developed a chart to help you discover where you're assertive and where you're nonassertive. By using this chart, you will be able to locate your weakest areas. That will help you develop a plan to make yourself more assertive in those areas.

RATE YOURSELF

In using the chart on page 119, you're to answer three questions for each box. Then place your answers in the box.

The answers for the first question are *usually, sometimes,*

ASSERTION SELF-ASSESSMENT TABLE

Behaviors   *People or Situations*

Behaviors	Commercial transactions	Authority figures	Co-workers	Church members	Immediate family	Parents, in-laws, other family	Children	Non-Christians	Christians	Friends of the opposite sex	Friends of the same sex
Giving compliments											
Receiving compliments											
Expressing affection											
Making requests											
Expressing personal opinions											
Refusing requests											
Standing up for legitimate rights											
Expressing moral values											
Witnessing											
Expressing disagreement											
Expressing displeasure or anger											

or *seldom.* You can answer the questions by inserting behavior and people or situations into the following pattern question: "Do I *(row heading)* to/from/of/with/in *(column heading)* when it is appropriate?" For example, using the first row and first column you would ask, "Do I *give compliments* in *commercial transactions* when it is appropriate?" The behavior is giving compliments, and the situation is a commercial transaction in which you are buying something from or selling something to another person. You would give one of the three answers listed above. You would then move across the top row, answering the question, "Do I give compliments . . . when it is appropriate?" about each of the people or situations listed in the columns.

To complete this portion of the exercise, examine the table when you've finished answering all the questions. Is there a pattern to your "sometimes" and "seldom" answers? For example, did you use "sometimes" or "seldom" in most of the columns expressing disagreement? It might be helpful to record the number of "sometimes" and "seldom" answers at the bottom of the table for each column and to the right of the table for each row. That would show you immediately which areas give you the most trouble, because those would have the highest totals. Those are the areas you need to work on.

I now want you to pose another question to the chart. I want to help you discover the situations in which you experience a high level of anxiety. This time a simple "yes" or "no" will be a sufficient answer. The pattern question is this: "When I *(row heading)* to/from/of/with/in *(column heading),* do I become very nervous or unduly anxious?" For example, beginning again with the first column and first row, "When I *give compliments* in *commercial transactions,* do I become very nervous or unduly anxious?" Complete the whole chart using this pattern. After you have done that, total the number of "yes" answers at the bottom and to the right of the chart. That will show you those behaviors, people, or situations that cause you the most anxiety. Those are the areas in which you should work at improvement.

Finally, I would like to help you discover situations in which you become angry. Again, a simple "yes" or "no" answer will be sufficient. The pattern question is this: "Am I aggressive when *(row heading)* to/from/of/with/in *(column heading)?*" When you have answered this question for each row heading and each column heading, total the "yes" answers at the bottom and the right side of the chart. That will show you those behaviors, people, or situations in which or with which you become aggressive. Those are the areas in which you should work at improvement.

To highlight the areas in which you have problems, you might want to shade lightly the squares representing those problems. That makes it easier for you to glance periodically at the chart to remember your problem areas.

CASE STUDIES

Now we come to the practical part, the hard part. At this point I want to help you develop plans to overcome your difficulties in being assertive. The best method for doing this (if you are working alone) is by writing. Select a situation and write out possible answers you might receive from a person in response to your particular behavior. You will create your own responses as a means of helping you overcome those situations in real life.

Ideally, assertiveness training should be roleplayed ahead of time. This means it's best if you can work with another person. In doing this, you describe for your partner the situation and behavior you want to practice. You make your statement (or the other person begins), and then you enter into a brief conversation. Frequently it's valuable to change places with your partner and play the role of the person with whom you have a hard time being assertive. By doing that a few times, you'll begin to develop the needed confidence to say the same sort of things in public rather than just in the practice situation.

I want to emphasize the importance of practicing with someone else. Although it's not impossible for a person to become more assertive while working alone, it's difficult. But when you've teamed yourself with another person to work on becoming more assertive, the possibilities for success will greatly multiply. Therefore, try to find someone to work with. That will make this exercise more valuable for you.

Because the chart contains eleven different behaviors and eleven different people or situations, I won't give examples of each. (You've already discovered that some behaviors and situations are not compatible, such as expressing affection during a commercial transaction.) Use the examples that are provided (there are twelve) as patterns for developing your own.

Situation 1—Giving compliments to authority figures
You have worked with a number of different supervisors over the years. Your present supervisor is one of the best, making your job much more enjoyable than it had often been in the past. You let him know that you appreciate his supervision.
Speaker: _____
Authority figure: It wasn't really much. I honestly think other men in the plant are doing as fine a job, probably better.
Speaker: _____
Authority figure: Well, thanks. I appreciate hearing that. It makes some of the rough times easier to handle.

Situation 2—Giving compliments to children
Your child has just painted a picture. You think it looks quite nice. Tell him so.
Speaker: _____
Child: No, it's not good. I sure messed it up in this corner by using the wrong color. Besides, John did a much better job than I did. He's the best.
Speaker: _____
Child: Do you really mean it? I don't like it. It didn't come out the way I wanted it to.
Speaker: _____

*Situation 3—Receiving compliments
from friends of the same sex*
During the past few months, your friend has had a number of serious problems. He lost his father, his wife had major surgery, and he had an accident with the car. He is expressing his appreciation for what you have done.
Friend: You have to be the best friend I've ever had. I really appreciate the way you've stood by me these last few months when things were really rough.

Speaker: _____
Friend: No, I mean it. Most people would not have done what you did. I don't think I could have made it without your support.
Speaker: _____

Situation 4—Expressing affection
to friends of the opposite sex
You have worked on a number of different projects at church with your friend. You have grown to have a deep appreciation for this person. Your affection is truly Christian and in no way romantic. With your spouse present you express your affection to the other person.
Speaker: _____
Friend: You're embarrassing me. You're putting me on.
Speaker: _____
Friend: You really mean that, don't you? Thanks. I appreciate it.

Situation 5—Making requests of a co-worker
You are having some difficulty with a new job you have been assigned. One of your co-workers has done this assignment on numerous occasions. You know you could do the job quicker if your co-worker would give you about an hour of his time. Ask for it.
Speaker: _____
Co-worker: I don't know. That would make it difficult for me to get my work done today.
Speaker: _____
Co-worker: All right, so long as you put it that way. Sure, I'll help.

Situation 6—Expressing personal opinions
to family members
You have just finished reading the newspaper. The article that interested you most dealt with the complexities of city hall and how difficult it is for the average citizen to get anything done. Your son also read the article and expresses an opinion to you. React.
Son: I think it's time someone did something about the

political situation in this town. Those guys who run the town don't have any idea what good government is. They should be run out of office.

Speaker: _____

Son: You don't really know what you're talking about. Did you hear that our mayor is being investigated by a grand jury? That proves they have no business in office.

Speaker: _____

*Situation 7—Refusing requests
from immediate family members*
Your spouse is active in the PTA and frequently asks you to join in the activities. A membership drive is on, and your spouse wants you to help her recruit a new member. React.

Spouse: I want you to come with me when I go talk to Shirley Ames about joining the PTA. I'm going right after supper.

Speaker: _____

Spouse: This is just as much your responsibility as mine. Your kids go to the school, too. Why do you help so rarely with the PTA?

Speaker: _____

*Situation 8—Standing up for legitimate rights
in a commercial transaction*
Last week you purchased a pair of pants on sale at a local department store. When you got home you saw that there was a flaw in one knee. You need to tell the clerk you want your money back or an exchange.

Speaker: _____

Store clerk: I'm sorry you're upset, but those items were on sale. Our store policy is that sale merchandise cannot be returned no matter what you discover when you get home.

Speaker: _____

Store clerk: If you aren't satisfied, that's too bad. You'll have to take it up with the manufacturer. We sell the stuff, we don't make it.

Speaker: _____

Situation 9—Expressing moral values to co-workers
In your department, everyone is given thirty minutes for

lunch and ten minutes for a coffee break. Over the years your co-workers have gotten into the habit of taking a forty minute lunch and a twenty minute coffee break. You're new in the department, and you've been taking only the allotted time. You need to defend your action.

Co-worker: You're messing things up for everyone else by coming back from lunch after only thirty minutes when everyone else takes forty. Why can't you cooperate? It doesn't hurt you to take more time.

Speaker: _____

Co-worker: What are you, some kind of prude? People have been taking forty minutes for lunch around here for years, and you're messing things up. Why be such a righteous troublemaker when bending a little would help us all?

Speaker: _____

Situation 10—Witnessing to a non-Christian
One of your fellow workers has been having some difficulty in his family. As you relate similar experiences you went through some years ago, you tell how Jesus Christ played a significant role in helping you through the difficulty.

Speaker: _____

Non-Christian: What do you mean, "You need Jesus"? Do you think I'm some kind of pagan or something?

Speaker: _____

Non-Christian: Well, I don't know about that. Besides, my religion is my business. I'd appreciate it if you would talk about something else.

Speaker: _____

Situation 11—Expressing disagreement with a Christian
In your Sunday school class, you related an experience you had the previous week. One of the other people in the class tells you that what you did was wrong. You try to show him why you think you were right.

Speaker: _____

Christian: Are you sure that's what the Bible says? That idea sounds a lot like the liberal, social gospel. We don't want any of that around here.

Speaker: _____

Christian: I still say that sounds liberal. I don't really think

you can support it with *proper* Bible interpretation. It contradicts so much of what I *know* to be right.
Speaker: _____

Situation 12—Expressing displeasure or anger with church members

Two weeks ago you asked one of the men in your church to do a job for you as part of the Christmas program preparation. He promised to have it done by last Saturday. Because it isn't done, you're way behind in getting the program ready. When you call to talk to him, he says he didn't get it done because he had more important things to do. You express your anger at his breaking his promise.
Speaker: _____
Church member: Oh, I didn't know you felt that way. I'm really surprised that such a little thing would upset you so. I always thought you were a better Christian than that.
Speaker: _____
Church member: Well, I'm glad you got it out. Something like that could cause trouble down the line. I didn't realize my failure would affect you like this. I still think you got upset over nothing.
Speaker: _____

In each of these situations, I've attempted to help you react to each of the different behaviors and people or situations at least once. While you were going through the situations, I hope you also picked up a pattern you can use for yourself. For example, let's assume that you can have difficulty making requests from co-workers. You can picture in your mind a situation in which you would have to make a request of a co-worker. You could then write down what you would say when you made the request, what your co-worker would say in response, and how you would answer, until you are satisfied with the exchange. You can do this a number of times with each situation. (You can also roleplay, as I suggested earlier.) In that way you can use what you've learned here in the future. Creating from your experience situations that cause you trouble can be a big help in giving you more confidence and helping you to behave more assertively. As I said, though, start small so that you can build on your successes.

THIRTEEN
The Assertive Witness

Would you like to be a more effective witness for Jesus Christ? Few Christians say no to that question. For most of us this is a major area of concern, frequently an area generating great guilt. You know you should be witnessing on a regular basis, but you also know you have led few, if any, people to a profession of faith in Jesus Christ. Every time you hear another sermon on witnessing, it simply generates more guilt.

If there is one area in which the principles of assertiveness training most urgently need application, it's in our Christian witness. This is one of two major concerns that originally interested me in assertiveness. So let's take all the different ideas you've picked up while reading this book and apply them to witnessing. Witnessing will then be our test case on the effectiveness of assertiveness training.

Three factors create the foundation for assertive witnessing. As with any treatment of witnessing, we begin with Jesus' commands (Acts 1:8; Matt. 28:19, 20). You don't witness because it is the assertive thing to do, but because you want to obey our Lord and Savior.

Assertiveness, however, presents to you two major building blocks for a witnessing foundation in addition to the biblical base. First, manipulation of others is wrong. Yet much witnessing falls into this category because we Christians are fearful about how people will respond.

When I was a college student, I worked with a large Christian organization attempting to win people to Christ. Once we held a softball game in the early evening as a come-on for an evangelistic chalk-talk after it got dark. We appealed to the teenagers to come to the softball game, never mentioning the chalk-talk. We also gave them transportation to the game, but we didn't plan to give them transportation home until after the evangelistic talk. That was manipulation! We tricked them. And they reacted very negatively. One even offered to beat me up for tricking him. So, as with any assertive response, you determine to give up any manipulation. You will be honest with people, never tricking them into hearing the gospel.

But we also learn about assertive witnessing in the assertive bill of rights. You have a right to your opinion. As you remember, this is the most basic right, the right all others come from. But doesn't our society say to you, "You don't have the right to talk to me about religion because that's my business, a private matter"? Certainly it does. But the bill of rights (not to mention the First Amendment to the Constitution) says you have the right to your opinion and to express that opinion. Being a Christian does not deprive you of that right. If that opinion doesn't agree with what others think, that's not your problem, but theirs. You have the right to your conviction that everyone needs to accept Jesus Christ as Savior and Lord of his life. You have the right to that opinion and to express it, even if it offends others.

But there's another side to this. You also have a responsibility. Your right to your opinion does not give you the right to force someone else to join you in that opinion. Many people think of witnessing as convincing another person *against his will* to accept Christ. Then, after the person has committed himself to Christ, he will realize how wonderful his decision really was. That's manipulation, not witnessing. Witnessing means that you express to another person your conviction of his need for Christ. Your responsibility both as a Christian and as another person is to respect his integrity. That means you can only present to him the evidence necessary for a decision. Should he decide to reject Christ, you must respect his decision. You might use active listening to clarify his rejection, but once it is clear, you accept it. You continue your witness at other times and places, but at all times you respect his integrity as a person and permit him to tell you, "I don't want Christ as my Savior." The decision is between him and God.

ANXIETY AND WITNESSING

Assertiveness training teaches us most about witnessing when it deals with overcoming anxiety. Right now I want you to lean back in your chair. Close your eyes. Now picture yourself giving a tract to a non-Christian acquaintance and asking him if he would like to accept Jesus Christ as his Savior and Lord. As you enter this experience, be sensitive to every emotion you experience. Write down those emotions.

What did you experience? Fear? Fear of rejection? Anxiety? But remember the SUDS score you used in determining your level of anxiety? Part of what you learned is that anxiety is normal in many situations in life. And anxiety is just as normal during witnessing as it would be if you were asked to give a talk to a group in your church. Anxiety is the unavoidable consequence of concern about your success. If you really want to lead a person to Christ through your witnessing, you will experience anxiety. But as in our earlier discussion, we must pose questions about its intensity.

What level of anxiety were you anticipating in the imaginary witnessing situation? Do you think that's the level you'll always experience? If you expect the level to drop, how far should it drop? What level of anxiety do you anticipate as normal for you when you're witnessing? Write it down.

Now let's deal assertively with your anxiety. You do this first of all by praying. The Bible tells us very clearly that anxiety is overcome through prayer (Phil. 4:6, 7). Don't take this as a pious aside. Prayer reduces anxiety.

However, in addition, assertiveness training gives you principles that will reduce your anxiety. Remember what was said concerning any situation in which you want to become more assertive: Prepare a conversation to use when you encounter that situation. The same applies to witnessing. Learn a planned approach, such as Campus Crusade for Christ's Four Spiritual Laws. This will reduce your anxiety.

Learn the approach using the various tools suggested by assertiveness training. *Practice* your witnessing plan with

Christian friends. That will reduce your anxiety about witnessing the first time to a non-Christian.

But let me introduce a caution. *Set a limit to your practice with Christian friends.* Some people would practice with Christian friends for the rest of their lives if they could to avoid ever talking to a non-Christian about Christ! I suggest no more than ten practice sessions with Christians.

While you're practicing with Christian friends, mentally select a non-Christian acquaintance for your first witnessing attempt. Begin now to pray for that person. Begin also to spend time with the person when you have no witnessing planned. This removes the tension that comes from feeling that you only want to be with this person to win him for Christ. You want to be with him because he is a creation of the living God, a fellow human being like yourself (I am assuming you *do* care for the person as more than just someone to win to Christ).

Let me elaborate on this idea of spending time with people other than when you want to witness to them. Part of our fear of witnessing comes from the fact that we "jump" on people who know little about us and about whom we know little. But if you spend time with a person, time other than when you want to witness, you demonstrate that you're interested in the person for reasons other than soulwinning, even if soulwinning is still your ultimate goal. But your witness then also comes out of the context of *your* life. The person knows what sort of person it is who is talking about Christ. Your soulwinning attempt then comes from the context of a living witness in which you have demonstrated by your actions that Christ has indeed changed your life. (Obviously, if you're serious about witnessing, you have to be committed to living a godly life. A hypocritical witness does not please God or have a favorable effect.)

Eventually, you're going to have to approach a non-Christian. Use your desire to learn how to witness to help you. Ask a non-Christian friend, "Can you help me? I want to learn how to discuss my faith in Christ more effectively. I'm learning a method for doing that, but I need someone to practice with. May I practice with you?"

Although this may sound like a strange way of learning

how to witness, I have reasons for suggesting it. But first, be careful! This situation is loaded with potential for manipulation. You're practicing. Don't use the occasion to sneak up on your non-Christian acquaintance and clobber him with the gospel.

Why do I want you to practice with a non-Christian friend? First, practicing with a non-Christian friend is a halfway step between practicing with a Christian friend and actually attempting to witness. Second, because your Christian friend knows the gospel well, he can't tell if you're having problems communicating. Your non-Christian friend is facing something new, and thus he can give you insight into the effectiveness of your presentation. Here you want to use active listening as you attempt to learn what faults you have in making your presentation. Don't be afraid to ask, "What am I asking you to do? Why do I want you to do it?" The answers will reveal the clarity of your presentation.

But there is a major problem here. Can you really lead a non-Christian acquaintance to the Living Water and not invite him to drink? No. You can't "just practice" presenting the gospel to a non-Christian. Thus, I would make this suggestion. When you've finished your presentation, conclude with a statement such as this: "I have presented the gospel to you because I needed to learn how to communicate it more effectively. I appreciate your help in letting me practice with you. I didn't do this to trick you into accepting Christ. But for me this message is so important that I can't simply tell it to you in practice without also asking, 'Would you like to accept Jesus Christ as your Savior?' I think I would be wrong not to at least ask you."

At this point, if the person says no, you have to respect his right to turn away. You don't want this to be a sneaky form of manipulation.

Let me give you another suggestion about reducing your anxiety level as you witness. Get together with a friend who is known as a good witness, and spend time with him in planned witnessing situations. That will do a number of things for you. It will show you that people don't always respond negatively to the gospel. It will also show you that people don't usually pose questions too hard for you to answer. Finally, it will demonstrate how easy and rewarding witnessing can be as you gain experience.

BEGINNING TO WITNESS

Now you are actually going to begin witnessing. Remember the principle of assertiveness that says, "Begin small and build on your success." Don't begin by witnessing to the most difficult person you know. Choose the person you think will give the least resistance to your witness. This does not necessarily mean he will accept Christ, but only that he will listen.

You began with the feeling, "Others might reject me if I witness to them." In your exploration of assertiveness training, you discovered that one method for overcoming anxiety is developing counterthoughts to overcome your negative thoughts. You learned that anxiety arises in part from what you tell yourself about what will happen when you witness. Let's examine this fear.

"Others might reject me if I witness to them." One way to develop counterthoughts is to put yourself in the other person's shoes. Let's do that. "How do I react when a person approaches me about joining a non-Christian cult? Do I reject him forever? Do I avoid him at all times in the future? Do I ban him from any and all gatherings where I am present? Do I spread evil rumors about him? No, not if my Christian faith means anything. I treat him as I would anyone else with the single exception that I recognize he has a religious belief that is in error. People I choose to witness to will probably react no differently from me."

Let's assume the worst. Let's assume that you witness and the person absolutely rejects you from that day on. What would that do to your life? Write out your answer.

My answer would be something like this: I would feel disappointed, possibly even hurt. But I would go on living. I would find other friends. Besides, if a person so completely rejects Jesus Christ, the most important Person in my life, I probably would not have much in common with him in the long run anyhow. Therefore, it's best that I discover that now rather than sometime down the road.

Another part of placing yourself in the other person's shoes is saying, "What sort of response can I anticipate?" Imagine the verbal response you will expect. What will you do if the person says, "Yes, I would like to hear what you have to say"? What will you do if the person says, "No, I'm not interested"? Will you stop right then? Or will you attempt a further response such as, "Would you mind telling me why?" "Would another time be more convenient?" Think out your responses to two or three different answers you might receive.

CHANGE

Change doesn't just happen; it's usually planned. That's a basic principle about assertiveness that we learned in Chapter 4. Now let's apply that to witnessing.

Create a plan for change. Remember that your Christian witness is a reflection of your basic personality. If you are outgoing with people, you will probably find it easier to become an effective witness. If you are quiet, somewhat retiring, highly sensitive to public opinion, you will become an effective witness more slowly. You should choose a method for witnessing that is most comfortable for you. If you are quiet and retiring, you probably don't want to plan on preaching on street corners. You might begin by explaining your faith in a letter to a friend and then discussing it at a later time. Choose a method that will create the least amount of anxiety for you, but begin somewhere.

Second, become confident with your witnessing tool, as I have already said.

Third, enlist a friend. I cannot begin to say enough about the value of a friend in encouraging growth in witnessing. I remember when I was in high school and three of us planned each week to get together to hand out tracts at local places popular with teens. By ourselves we witnessed only sporadically, but each weekend we witnessed with some effect because we had the social pressure and support that came from working with friends. So don't plan to become an effective witness by yourself. Enlist the aid of a friend—if possible, a friend who is already effective as a witness.

Establish a level for success that is appropriate for you. A major problem people face in witnessing is the preacher who says, "I make it my practice to witness to at least one person each day." Great! More power to him! If I worked at that level I would have ulcers, bite all my fingernails off, and be constantly on edge. I choose a plan that brings me into regular contact with non-Christians so that when opportunity arises, I can witness to them of their need to believe in Christ as Savior.

Your plan for success might run something like this: "I will attend one meeting each month (week) at which non-Christians are present. Once every three months, I will attempt to create a situation in which I can tell one of those people how to become a Christian. I will attempt to take advantage of whatever spontaneous witnessing opportunities arise."

Now you have a target for success. Measure yourself based on that target, not on what someone else is doing. Remember, you learned in developing a positive self-image that you can't base your life on comparisons with other people. Your built-in tendency is to downgrade yourself. Plan for yourself.

Now you come to the most crucial point of all—*beginning*. Unless you begin, all the planning in the world is worth nothing. What day are you going to start? Write it down. Keep it.

IS NOW THE TIME OR THE PLACE?

"Should I witness now? Would it really be appropriate? Would another time be better? How would he react if I witnessed now?"

These questions always face you as you think about witnessing. You never quite know what to do. If you're like me, many times you solve the problem by doing nothing—but then you feel guilty when the occasion is gone. If you plan a special time for witnessing, you will not entirely overcome your anxiety, but you will create a situation that will help you act in spite of your anxiety.

Let me inject a thought here that could really change your witnessing. Be open to making mistakes. No matter how good a witness you are, you will sometimes begin witnessing when the time or place is inappropriate. Don't worry about it! You simply apologize and wait for another opportunity. Your friend will have more respect for you in the future, because you treated him as a person worthy of respect rather than as a soul whose scalp you want to hang on your evangelistic belt.

Planned witnessing opportunities provide the best opportunity for you to learn how to be an effective witness. If you go to a friend's house where you plan to witness or invite a friend over to your house and plan to witness, you will reduce your level of anxiety.

I've already mentioned the value—the necessity—of meeting non-Christians in a context other than when you plan to witness to them. I want now to expand on that idea. You can't witness effectively unless you get to know people by regular contact with them. (There are exceptions, but this is a good general rule.) This means that for most Christians you have to plan times and places where you will meet non-Christians. Our churches often keep us so busy we simply don't have time for regular contacts with non-Christians. Thus, meeting them may take planning and effort on your part. It might even mean missing an occasional church activity to be with non-Christians. But try this. Think about your favorite hobby, sport, leisure-time activity, or social interest. Is there a club in your neighborhood that caters to your interest? Why not join it? You would enjoy learning more about the activity, and you would also be meeting non-Christians with similar interests, thus generating witnessing opportunities.

As an avid fisherman, I fish by the principle that I will catch more fish in a stream than by fishing in my backyard. Elementary as that may sound, we can turn it into a spiritual thought by stating, "You'll win more people to Christ by going to them than by waiting for them to come to you." If all your friends and acquaintances are Christians, you'll have few witnessing opportunities, but if you plan time with non-Christians, you'll have more witnessing opportunities.

Let's imagine that you have a friend you want to witness to. How do you get him into the house for a witnessing opportunity? First, you begin by giving up all thoughts of manipulation. You let him know what you plan to do by a statement something like this: "George, could you come over to the house after dinner Friday night for dessert? I have something important I would like to discuss with you. I'd like to tell you how Jesus Christ has given meaning to my life. Could you make it?" You honestly tell him what you plan without giving him so much detail that you frighten him off. Any questions he might pose about the subject matter for the evening can be set aside with, "This isn't really the time or the place to discuss the subject. I would really prefer the more relaxed atmosphere of my home." (You could also use a restaurant, with you, of course, paying the bill.) But in all of this you seek honesty without detailed explanation.

Your friend is now in your home. You begin to witness to him. But he has some negative reactions while remaining basically open. What should you do? Remember, we saw that conflict is not necessarily bad. How often have you been told, "Don't argue religion; it will just destroy the witness." Well, that's true—but only partially. If it becomes an argument in which people are becoming angry, that will destroy the witness. But many times we fail because we don't realize the need for a healthy exchange of opinions on the way to a person's becoming a Christian—possibly five years from now. Conflict that is not arguing is good.

But make sure you use active listening. Many non-Christians lose all interest in Christ because Christians act as though they have all the answers. We Christians often don't really listen to what they say; we just wait with our answer until they are finished, then jump them with the *truth*. That's wrong. You need to pay attention, and active listening is the best tool for that purpose.

Many times, if you will take the time to listen to what a non-Christian is saying, you will discover a real problem, not just some false front designed to put you off. In addition, listening involves hearing more than words; it involves hearing emotions. For example, take the question, "Will all the people who have never heard about Christ be condemned to hell?" The theologically correct answer is an unequivocal yes. But that does not hear the person's feelings. Think about it yourself for a moment. That means that billions of people will perish for all eternity without ever responding to—even hearing—the gospel. That's tragic! If a hurricane that kills thousands provokes our sympathy, how much more this tragedy. Thus I'd answer, "I really feel what you are saying. You see that as a tremendous loss, a tragedy of unbelievable proportions. I have to agree. And that's the way God feels, too. He says he is unwilling that any should perish. Since he is both a loving and a just God, I don't know how he will work that out, but I have to believe that his compassion is greater than ours will ever be. The Bible appears to say they will perish, but let's rest our faith in God, who loves men with perfect justice." I don't avoid the question, but I hear the emotions as well as the words. Active listening can be an effective tool in evangelism.

The same goes for I-messages. How often an evangelistic encounter has been spoiled when a Christian confidently states, "You're wrong. The Bible says ⁻ ." After making certain through active listening that you have heard what he is saying, you can respond, "I think the Bible says. . . . What do you think?" Or you might say, "I think differently about that. Here's what I think. . . ." These statements place no blame or guilt on the other person, but leave him the opportunity to retain his self-respect. You are not attacking him or his views, but explaining what you believe.

CRITERIA FOR APPROPRIATENESS

Now we come to the most important question most people face. "How can I tell whether it's appropriate to witness or not?" Given the complexity of the human personality, no one can answer that question for you. There are no rules that will show you what to do in every situation, but there are guidelines that will cover most situations.

Before we consider the guidelines, however, be honest with yourself. Learn to know when you are acting out of guilt, feelings of anxiety, or feelings of ignorance. Are you not witnessing because you would feel guilty about forcing your opinion on someone else?

Are you not witnessing because you don't like the feeling of anxiety that goes along with witnessing? Are you afraid someone might ask you a question you couldn't answer? Deep down, would you be embarrassed or ashamed to admit you're a Christian? These clues show you the problem to face. At that point, you have to determine whether you want to witness in spite of those feelings.

First among the guidelines, will witnessing demonstrate

concern for the other person? Or are you simply concerned about getting your own way? This applies as much to witnessing as to anything else. Witnessing can be an attempt on your part to look good with your Christian friends by winning someone to Christ. Or it can be an act of loving concern for a person who needs Christ.

Second, you need to be sensitive to God's Spirit in these situations. If time permits, a quick prayer for guidance would be appropriate. If not, you always have the Holy Spirit working within you to guide you in making these decisions. You need to be conscious of his activity and to be willing to speak as he directs. This applies particularly to sensing whether a person is open to your witness. Fears and anxieties may often keep you from sensing that your non-Christian friend is indeed open, even eager, to hear what you have to say.

Loving concern demands that you consider the matter of time or the situation you're in. Sometimes you need simply to listen to what another person is saying without any immediate response, because the situation prohibits effective communication. You can't witness everywhere. At other times, the freedom of the situation might suggest that this is an excellent time for witness. Contrast, for example, a situation in which children are fighting all around you as they have a bad day, and a discussion in a quiet spot in a restaurant when you and your friend have ample time. Thus, timing *is* a consideration.

Analyze your friend's situation. All of us are most open to other people's advice during times of crisis or stress in our lives. Although those are not the only times for witnessing, they are particularly appropriate times to tell how Christ has helped you in similar situations in the past. Active listening helps you enter into the other person's pain by showing understanding of how he is hurting, but it also opens the door to discuss actively the need to accept Christ. Thus, while much of what I have said about appropriateness relates to your feelings, I must emphasize the obvious fact that the other person's needs and circumstances should dominate your thinking. You should not focus on your feelings so much that you fail to see another person's need.

Next, recognize the naturalness of feelings of anxiety. If

you are going to assert yourself, anxiety is natural. If you plan on witnessing to a person, you will feel anxiety. But that should not prevent you from doing what needs to be done. The whole purpose of this book is to convince you that you should often act in spite of feelings of anxiety, because that is best for everyone.

Deal, then, with realistic fears or worries. You might fear that if you witness on the job you will be fired. Deal with that fear. In some places it might be completely true. Then you have to determine whether witnessing on the job is the wisest thing for you, given other priorities (the need to support your family) and opportunities (you can witness after work) in your life. But possibly you would just have to deal with the timing on the job. Witnessing while working would be grounds for dismissal, but what you say during your lunch break would have no effect. Examine and deal with your fears. Think through the consequences; pray and study your Bible; then act as you think God would want you to.

Finally, and I can't emphasize this enough, *be open to mistakes.* Key to any Christian assertive behavior is freedom to admit failure. This applies to witnessing as much as to anything else. Be quick to say with sincerity, "I'm sorry. I didn't intend to intrude." "I was wrong in pushing as I did. Would you forgive me?" "I didn't realize how concerned you were about. . . . Forgive me for placing my concerns above yours." Assertive behavior is no cure-all for interpersonal relationships. You will err. That I can guarantee. But if you admit your mistakes and move on from there, you will become more and more open and feel far better about yourself, thus improving your witness.

I've attempted to deal with what I think is a major problem in witnessing, people's feelings. People's negative feelings keep them from witnessing, possibly more than anything else. But there's another side to witnessing that we can't overlook—in the end, your feelings really don't matter. That may sound like a total contradiction of all I've said, but it isn't really.

It's important to deal with your feelings because they affect the way you witness. But as a Christian you have an obligation to witness no matter what your feelings. You cannot ignore the Great Commission. A person who witnesses while all tied up inside with anxiety is at least obedient; a person who never witnesses is disobedient. At least the first person is trying to do God's will. Deal with your feelings, certainly, but if you can't get your feelings under control, go out and witness with all the feelings of anxiety and fear still operating. God will go with you if your motive is to please him. Nothing in this chapter should encourage you to think you don't have to witness if you don't have the right feelings.